Laboratory Manual

CONCEPTS AND CHALLENGES

EARTH ❖ SCIENCE

Martin Schachter ◆ Alan Winkler ◆ Stanley Wolfe

Stanley Wolfe
Project Coordinator

GLOBE FEARON
Pearson Learning Group

The following people have contributed to the development of this product:

Art and Design: Evelyn Bauer, Susan Brorein, Tracey Gerber, Bernadette Hruby, Carol Marie Kiernan, Mindy Klarman, Judy Mahoney, Karen Mancinelli, Elbaliz Mendez, April Okano, Dan Thomas, Jennifer Visco

Editorial: Stephanie P. Cahill, Gina Dalessio, Nija Dixon, Martha Feehan, Theresa McCarthy, Maurice Sabean, Marilyn Sarch, Maury Solomon, S. Adrienn Vegh-Soti, Shirley C. White, Jeffrey Wickersty

Manufacturing: Mark Cirillo, Tom Dunne

Marketing: Douglas Falk, Stephanie Schuler

Production: Irene Belinsky, Linda Bierniak, Carlos Blas, Karen Edmonds, Cheryl Golding, Leslie Greenberg, Roxanne Knoll, Susan Levine, Cynthia Lynch, Jennifer Murphy, Lisa Svoronos, Susan Tamm

Publishing Operations: Carolyn Coyle, Thomas Daning, Richetta Lobban

Technology: Ellen Strain

About the Cover: Earth science is the study of Earth and its history. The images of the Grand Canyon and running water represent some of the things students will be learning in this book. Erosion caused by running water helped to create the Grand Canyon. The rock layers of the Grand Canyon provide Earth scientists with an opportunity to study millions of years of geologic history of this region of North America. What do you think are some of the other things you will study in Earth science?

ISBN: 0-13-023847-3

Printed in the United States of America

4 5 6 7 8 9 10   06 05 04

Globe Fearon
Pearson Learning Group

1-800-321-3106
www.pearsonlearning.com

CONTENTS

SAFETY IN THE SCIENCE LABORATORY

Unlike many other fields of study, science allows you an opportunity to "learn by doing." Part of this process often involves work both in the laboratory and in the field.

Working a science laboratory can be both exciting and meaningful. However, when carrying out experiments, you may sometimes work with materials that can be dangerous if not handled properly. For this reason, you must always be aware of proper safety procedures. You can avoid accidents in the laboratory by following a few simple guidelines:

- **Always** handle all material carefully.
- **Never** perform a laboratory investigation without direction from your teacher.
- **Never** work alone in the science laboratory.
- **Always** read directions in a laboratory investigation before beginning the laboratory.

Throughout this laboratory program, you will see the safety symbols that are shown below and on the next page. Before beginning any laboratory, be sure to read the laboratory and note any safety symbols and caution statements. If you know what each symbol means, and always follow the guidelines that apply to each symbol, your work in the laboratory will be both safe and exciting.

SAFETY SYMBOLS

Clothing Protection
- Wear your laboratory apron to protect your clothing from stains or burns.

Eye Safety
- Wear your laboratory goggles, especially when working with open flames and chemicals.
- If chemicals get into your eyes, flush your eyes with plenty of water. Notify your teacher immediately.
- Be sure you know how to use the emergency eyewash system in the laboratory.

Clean Up
- Always wash your hands after an activity in which you handle chemicals, animals, or plants.

Disposal
- Keep your work area clean at all times.
- Dispose of all materials properly. Follow your teacher's instructions for disposal.

Glassware Safety
- Handle glassware carefully.
- Check all glassware for chips or cracks before using it. Never use glassware that has chips or cracks.
- Do not try to clean up broken glassware. Notify your teacher if you break a piece of glassware.
- Air-dry all glassware. Do not use paper towels to dry glassware.
- Never force glass tubing into the hole of a rubber stopper.

Heating Safety
- Be careful when handling hot objects.
- Turn off the hot plate or other heat source when you are not using it.
- When you heat chemicals in a test tube, always point the test tube away from people.

Fire Safety

- Confine loose clothing and tie back long hair when working near an open flame.
- Be sure you know the location of fire extinguishers and fire blankets in the laboratory.
- Never reach across an open flame.

Dangerous Chemicals

- Use extreme care when working with acids and bases. Both acids and bases can cause burns. If you spill an acid or a base on your skin, flush your skin with plenty of water. Notify your teacher immediately.
- Never mix chemicals unless you are instructed to do so by your teacher.
- Never pour water into an acid or a base. Always pour an acid or a base into water.
- Never smell anything directly.
- Use caution when handling chemicals that produce fumes.

Poison

- Never use chemicals without directions from your teacher.
- Use all poisonous chemicals with extreme caution.
- Inform your teacher immediately if you spill chemicals or get any chemicals in your eyes or on your skin.

Sharp Objects

- Be careful when using scissors, scalpels, knives, or other cutting instruments.
- Always dissect specimens in a dissecting pan. Never dissect a specimen while holding it in your hand.
- Always cut in the direction away from your body.

Electrical Safety

- Check all electrical equipment for loose plugs or worn cords before using it.
- Be sure that electrical cords are not placed where people can trip over them.
- Do not use electrical equipment with wet hands or near water.
- Never overload an electrical circuit.

Plant Safety

- Never eat any part of a plant that you cannot identify as edible.
- Some plants, such as poison ivy, are harmful if they are touched or eaten. Use caution when handling or collecting plants. Always use a reliable field guide to plants.

Animal Safety

- Be careful when handling live animals. Some animals can injure you or spread disease.
- Do not bring live animals into class that have not been purchased from a reputable pet store.

Caution

- Follow the ⚠ CAUTION and safety symbols you see used throughout this manual when doing labs or other activities.

EARTH SCIENCE EQUIPMENT AND APPARATUS

As you work in the earth science laboratory, you will need to become familiar with many pieces of equipment and apparatus. Several common pieces of equipment are shown below and on the next page. Below the name of each piece of equipment is a brief description of what the equipment is used for.

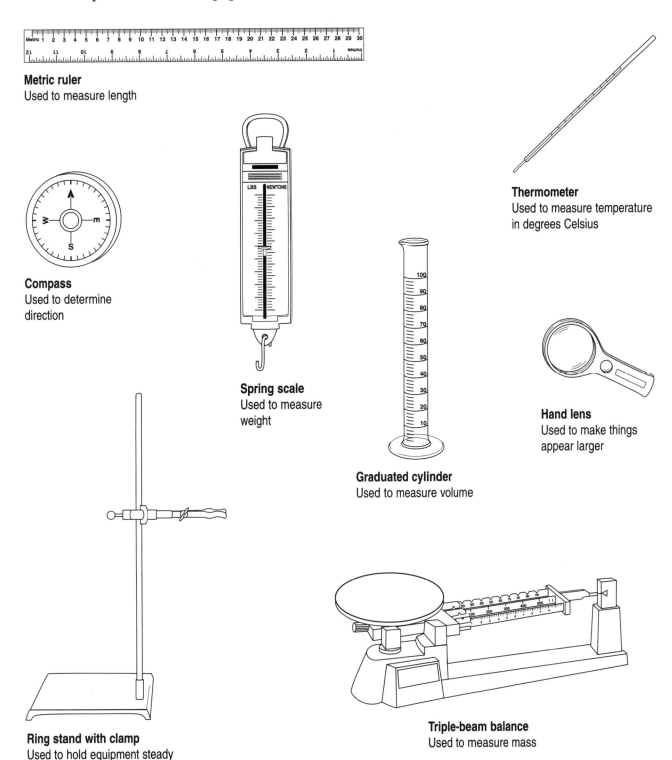

Metric ruler
Used to measure length

Compass
Used to determine direction

Spring scale
Used to measure weight

Graduated cylinder
Used to measure volume

Thermometer
Used to measure temperature in degrees Celsius

Hand lens
Used to make things appear larger

Ring stand with clamp
Used to hold equipment steady

Triple-beam balance
Used to measure mass

EARTH SCIENCE EQUIPMENT AND APPARATUS

Funnel and tripod
Used to hold materials through which water trickles

Dropper
Used to add small amounts of liquids

Diffraction grating
Used to separate light

Stirring rod
Used to mix materials

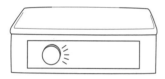

Hot plate
Used to heat materials

Beakers
Used to hold materials

Test tube holder
Used to hold hot test tubes

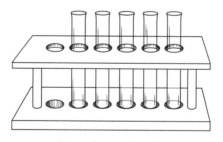

Test tubes and rack
Used to hold materials

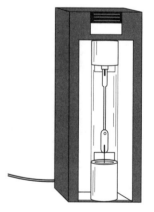

Gas vapor tube
Used to produce a spectrum for certain elements

Name _____ Class _____ Date _____

LABORATORY SKILLS WORKSHEET 1

Using a Graduated Cylinder

Materials

100-mL graduated
cylinder

dropper

small jar

BACKGROUND: A graduated cylinder is used to measure the volume of a liquid. A graduated cylinder is a long tube marked along its side with lines that show the volume. Some graduated cylinders are small and measure only up to 10 milliliters of liquid. Others are larger and measure 25 milliliters, 100 milliliters, or more. Notice the 10-milliliter graduated cylinder in Figure 1. The long lines below the numbers show milliliters. The shorter lines show two-tenths of a milliliter. Other graduated cylinders may have different values for the long and short lines. When you pour a liquid into a graduated cylinder, you can use these lines to determine the volume of the liquid.

PURPOSE: In this activity, you will learn how to use a graduated cylinder.

PROCEDURE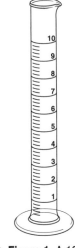

Part A: Reading a Graduated Cylinder

☐ 1. **OBSERVE:** Look at a graduated cylinder. Notice the markings on the side. The markings on a graduated cylinder are usually given in milliliters, which is abbreviated mL. Record information about this graduated cylinder in Table 1 on page 6.

☐ 2. Look at the graduated cylinder shown in Figure 2. Notice that the surface of the liquid is curved upward at the sides. This curve is called a meniscus. When you read the volume of a liquid in a graduated cylinder, you must look at it from eye level. Always read the volume at the flat, center part of the meniscus. In Figure 2, the volume is 8.6 mL.

☐ 3. Look at the graduated cylinder readings in Figure 3. Write the volume of the liquid in each graduated cylinder in the space provided.

▲ **Figure 1** A 10-mL graduated cylinder

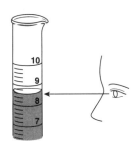

▲ **Figure 2** Reading the meniscus of a liquid in a graduated cylinder

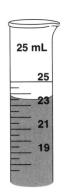 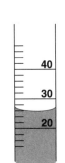 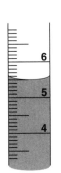 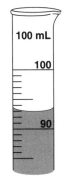

1. _____ 2. _____ 3. _____ 4. _____

▲ **Figure 3** Write the volume of liquid in each graduated cylinder.

Part B: Measuring the Volume of a Liquid

☐ 1. **MEASURE:** Half fill a small jar with water. Pour the water into the graduated cylinder. Record the volume of the water in Table 2. Ask your teacher to check your answer. Empty your graduated cylinder.

☐ 2. Repeat Step 4 two more times. Have your lab partner check your answers.

☐ 3. **MEASURE:** Use a graduated cylinder to measure 64 mL of water. First, fill the jar with water. Pour water from the jar into the graduated cylinder until it is between the 60 and 70-mL mark. Look at the meniscus from eye level. If the reading is greater than 64 mL, pour some of the water back into the jar. If the reading is less than 64 mL, use a dropper to get water from the jar and add it to the graduated cylinder. Continue until the lower part of the meniscus is on the 64-mL line.

☐ 4. Repeat Step 3 to measure 82 mL and 93 mL. Have your lab partner check your readings each time.

OBSERVATIONS

Table 1: Information About the Graduated Cylinder	
Greatest volume it will measure	
Volume shown by the longest lines	
Volume shown by the shortest lines	

Table 2: Reading a Graduated Cylinder	
Volume 1	
Volume 2	
Volume 3	

CONCLUSIONS

1. **COMPARE:** What is an advantage of measuring a liquid with a graduated cylinder instead of a beaker? _____

_____

2. **INFER:** If the smallest markings on a graduated cylinder are 1 mL apart, is it possible to measure a volume of 63.5 mL? Explain your answer.

_____

_____

3. Suppose that the long markings on a graduated cylinder are 1 mL apart and there are four short lines between the 8-mL and the 9-mL marks. What volumes do the short lines indicate?

_____

_____

Concepts and Challenges in Earth Science, Laboratory Manual © Pearson Education, Inc./Globe Fearon/Pearson Learning Group. All rights reserved. Copying strictly prohibited.

LABORATORY SKILLS WORKSHEET 2

Using a Triple-Beam Balance

BACKGROUND: Triple-beam balances are often used to find the mass of solid objects or powdered solids. Most triple-beam balances have a balance pan, three beams, a pointer, and a three-part scale with riders. Many balances also have an adjustment knob. The scale of a balance measures grams. The scale of the top beam gives readings in 10-gram intervals, for example, 10 grams, 20 grams, and so on, up to 100 grams. The scale of the middle beam gives readings in hundreds of grams. The scale of the bottom beam gives readings in grams from 1 gram to 10 grams. Each 1-gram interval shows tenths of a gram, from 0.1 gram to 0.9 gram. A triple-beam balance measures the mass of an object by balancing the mass in the pan with the riders on the scale.

PURPOSE: In this activity, you will learn how to use a triple-beam balance.

> ### Materials
> solid object
> 150-mL beaker
> salt
> tablespoon
> triple-beam balance

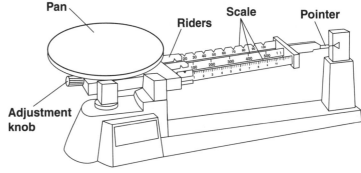

PROCEDURE

Part A: Reading a Mass

❑ 1. To read the mass of an object, read the position of the hundreds, tens, and ones riders to find the mass in hundreds, tens, ones, and tenths of grams. Read the mass shown on the triple-beam balance scale below.

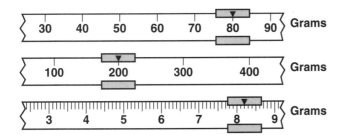

Table 1: Reading a Mass	
Rider	**Mass**
Tens rider	
Hundreds rider	
Ones rider	
Total mass	

❑ 2. **RECORD:** Record the mass shown by each rider in Table 1. Make sure that you write a decimal point before the number of tenths shown on the ones rider.

❑ 3. Add the masses together to find the total mass. Record this in Table 1.

Part B: Finding the Mass of a Solid Object

❑ 1. Before using a triple-beam balance, make sure that the balance is centered properly. Set all the riders to zero. The balance pointer should rest at the zero mark at the end of the scale. If the balance pointer is not at zero, turn the adjustment knob until the pointer arrives at zero.

❏ **2.** Place the object on the balance pan.

❏ **3. MEASURE:** Slide the riders until the pointer is once again on zero. This means that the scale is balanced. If the mass of the object is less than 10 grams, you will find that you do not need to move the top rider. If the mass of the object is less than 100 grams, you will not need to move the middle rider.

❏ **4. RECORD:** To find the mass of the object, first record the measurement shown on each of the three riders. Record this information in Table 2. Then, add the masses of each rider to find the total mass. Record your measurement in Table 2.

Part C: Finding the Mass of a Substance

❏ **1. MODEL:** Place a beaker on the balance pan to find its mass. Record this mass in Table 3.

❏ **2. MEASURE:** Place 1 tablespoon of salt in the beaker. Find the mass of the beaker and the salt combined. Record the mass in Table 3.

❏ **3. CALCULATE:** To find the mass of the salt alone, subtract the mass of the beaker from the combined mass of the beaker and salt. Record the mass of the salt in Table 3.

OBSERVATIONS

Table 2: Reading a Mass	
Rider	Mass
Tens rider	
Hundreds rider	
Ones rider	
Total mass	

Table 3: Finding the Mass of a Substance	
Mass of beaker (a)	
Mass of beaker plus salt (b)	
Total mass (b minus a)	

CONCLUSIONS

1. **CALCULATE:** What is the greatest mass that most triple-beam balances can accurately measure? _____

2. **INFER:** If only the ones rider needs to be moved from zero to balance a mass on the the balance pan, what is the largest mass that the object can have? _____

3. **INFER:** If the hundreds rider is left at zero and the tens and ones riders are moved to balance the scale, what is the largest mass that the object in the balance pan can have?

_____

LABORATORY SKILLS WORKSHEET 3

Measuring Volume and Density

Concepts and Challenges in Earth Science, Laboratory Manual © Pearson Education, Inc./Globe Fearon/Pearson Learning Group. All rights reserved. Copying strictly prohibited.

BACKGROUND: When you blow up a balloon, you force air into the balloon. The volume of the balloon must increase because the air takes up space. Volume is the amount of space that matter takes up. If you hold the balloon in one hand and hold a ball of the same size in your other hand, you notice that the ball is heavier. This is because the density of the ball is greater than that of the balloon. Density is the amount of matter in a given volume.

PURPOSE: In this activity, you will learn how to measure the volumes and densities of different solids and liquids.

PROCEDURE

Part A: Mass and Volume of a Rectangular Solid

☐ 1. Use a metric ruler to measure the length, width, and height of a wooden block. Use a wax pencil to label this block *1*. Record your measurements in Table 1 on page 11.

☐ 2. **CALCULATE:** Calculate the volume of block 1, using the following formula.

   Volume = length × width × height

   Record the volume in Table 1 and in Table 3.

☐ 3. Label the other wooden block *2*. Label the remaining rectangular solids *3* and *4*. In the spaces provided in Tables 1 and 3, indicate what materials solids 3 and 4 are made of.

☐ 4. Repeat Steps 1 and 2 for wooden block 2 and for solids 3 and 4.

☐ 5. Use a triple-beam balance to measure the masses of the wooden blocks and the other rectangular solids. Record the measurements in Table 3.

Part B: Mass and Volume of a Liquid

☐ 1. **MEASURE:** Use the balance to measure the mass of an empty 150-mL beaker. Record the measurement here.

   mass of beaker = _____ g

☐ 2. **MEASURE:** Half fill the beaker with water. Place it on the balance and measure the mass of the beaker and water together. Find the mass of the water, using the following formula.

   Mass (water) = mass (beaker + water) − mass (beaker)

   Record the mass of the water in Table 3.

Materials

100-mL graduated
   cylinder

150-mL beaker

2 rectangular solids of
   the same dimensions
   but different
   materials

2 rectangular wooden
   blocks of different
   dimensions

rubbing alcohol

wax pencil

metric ruler

small rock

triple-beam balance

❏ 3. Pour the water from the beaker into the graduated cylinder. Measure the volume of the water. Remember to read the volume by looking at the bottom of the meniscus. Record the measurement in Table 3.

❏ 4. Empty the graduated cylinder. Pour the same amount of rubbing alcohol as you had water into the graduated cylinder. Record the volume of rubbing alcohol in Table 3.

❏ 5. Pour the rubbing alcohol into the beaker. Use the balance to measure the mass of the rubbing alcohol and beaker together. Use the formula in Step 2 to find the mass of the rubbing alcohol. Record the mass of the alcohol in Table 3.

Part C: Mass and Volume of an Irregular Solid

❏ 1. Half fill the graduated cylinder with water. Read the volume of the water. Record the measurement in Table 2.

❏ 2. Carefully lower a small rock into the water in the graduated cylinder. The water level should rise. Read the level of the water. Record the volume of the water and rock in Table 2.

❏ 3. Find the volume of the rock, using the following formula.

Volume (rock) = volume (water + rock) – volume (water)

Because 1 mL = 1 cm^3, you can express the volume of the rock in cm^3.

❏ 4. Record the volume of the rock in Table 2 and Table 3.

❏ 5. Use the balance to find the mass of the rock. Record the mass in Table 3.

Part D: Density

❏ 1. **CALCULATE:** Calculate the density of wooden block 1, using the following formula.

Density = mass (g) ÷ volume (cm^3)

Record the density in Table 3.

❏ 2. Repeat Step 1 for wooden block 2, rectangular solids 3 and 4, and the rock.

❏ 3. Calculate the density of water, using the following formula.

Density = mass (g) ÷ volume (mL)

Record the density in Table 3.

❏ 4. Repeat Step 3 for the rubbing alcohol.

LABORATORY SKILLS WORKSHEET 3 (continued)

OBSERVATIONS

Table 1: Volumes of Rectangular Solids				
Item	Length	Width	Height	Volume
Wooden block 1				cm³
Wooden block 2				cm³
Solid 3 _____				cm³
Solid 4 _____				cm³

Table 2: Volume of an Irregular Solid	
Object	Volume
Water	_____ mL
Water + rock	_____ mL
Rock alone	_____ mL = _____ cm³

Table 3: Mass, Volume, and Density			
Substance	Mass	Volume	Density
Wooden block 1	g	cm³	g/cm³
Wooden block 2	g	cm³	g/cm³
Solid 3 _____	g	cm³	g/cm³
Solid 4 _____	g	cm³	g/cm³
Water	g	cm³	g/cm³
Rubbing alcohol	g	cm³	g/cm³
Rock	g	cm³	g/cm³

1. Which wooden block has the greater volume? Which has the greater mass?

   _____

2. How do the densities of the two wooden blocks compare? _____

   _____

3. Which rectangular solid—3 or 4—has the greater density? _____

4. Which liquid—water or rubbing alcohol—has the greater density? _____

CONCLUSIONS

5. How is the volume of a rectangular solid measured? _____

   _____

6. How is the volume of a liquid measured? _____

   _____

7. How is the volume of an irregular solid measured? Why is this method necessary?

   _____

   _____

   _____

8. Can two solids with the same volume have different densities? Explain your

   answer. _____

   _____

9. Can two solids made of the same substance have different densities? Explain

   your answer. _____

   _____

10. **COMPARE:** If you filled a 1-L bottle with water and another 1-L bottle with rubbing

    alcohol, which bottle would feel heavier? Why? _____

    _____

    _____

Name _____ Class _____ Date _____

LABORATORY SKILLS WORKSHEET 4

Organizing and Analyzing Data

Materials

paper
pencil

BACKGROUND: Data collected during experiments is not very useful unless it is easy to read and understand. Therefore, scientists often use tables to organize data. A table can display a lot of information in a small space. A table also makes it easy to compare and interpret data. Some tables, such as the one in Figure 1, are very simple and show only a small amount of data. Other tables, such as the one on page 14, are more complex. The type of table you use depends on your data.

PURPOSE: In this activity, you will learn to make and use tables.

PROCEDURE

☐ 1. Scientists have been keeping records of the location, size, and strength of earthquakes for many years. The Richter scale has been used worldwide to describe earthquake magnitude. Figure 2 shows some data collected from records describing some major earthquakes of the 20th century. (R = Richter scale) Think about how this data could be organized into a table.

☐ 2. **ORGANIZE:** Look at Table 1 on page 14. Like all tables, it has a title. Each column has a heading, and the headings show units for the data. Use the data from the records in Figure 2 to complete the table.

Major United States Earthquakes	
Year	**Location**
1811–1812	New Madrid, Missouri
1886	Charleston, South Carolina
1906	San Francisco, California
1964	Alaska
1971	San Francisco, California
1989	San Francisco Bay, California
1994	Northridge, California

▲ **Figure 1** A simple table

Quetta, Pakistan, 1978, 7.7R	Southern Alaska, 1964, 8.4R
Sakhalin, Russia, 1995, 7.5R	San Francisco, 1906, 8.3R
Kuril Islands, Russia, 1994, 7.9R	San Francisco, 1989, 6.9R
Tokyo, Japan, 1923, 8.3R	Los Angeles, 1994, 6.6R
Kobe, Japan, 1995, 7.2R	Mexico City, 1985, 8.1R
Bhuj, India, 2001, 6.9R	Guatemala, 1976, 7.5R
Izmit, Turkey, 1999, 7.4R	Chimbote, Peru, 1970, 7.8R
Flores, Indonesia, 1992, 7.5R	Naples, Italy, 1922, 7.2R

▲ **Figure 2** Earthquake data

OBSERVATIONS

Table 1: Major Earthquakes Worldwide					
Year	Location	Magnitude	Year	Location	Magnitude
	San Francisco			Mexico City	
	Naples, Italy			San Francisco	
	Tokyo, Japan			Flores, Indonesia	
	Southern Alaska			Kuril Islands, Russia	
	Chimbote, Peru			Los Angeles	
	Guatemala			Izmit, Turkey	
	Quetta, Pakistan			Bhuj, India	
	Sakhalin, Russia			Kobe, Japan	

1. In what year did the earliest major earthquake recorded in this listing take place? _____

2. In what year did the most recent major earthquake in this listing occur? _____

CONCLUSIONS

3. According to this data, what magnitude on the Richter scale is considered to be

   a major earthquake? _____

4. **ANALYZE:** Has major earthquake activity increased or decreased over the past

   100 years? _____

5. Explain how the table made it easier for you to answer the questions you have

   answered so far. _____

   _____

6. **ORGANIZE:** Think about the information in the table describing the earthquakes.
   How should the table look if you want to separate the earthquakes with a
   magnitude of 8.0 and higher from those below 8.0? On a separate sheet of paper,
   make a table that shows the data in this way.

LABORATORY SKILLS WORKSHEET 5

Graphing

> *Materials*
>
> colored pencils

BACKGROUND: Graphs are a useful way to organize and present information. Graphing data helps you see similarities and patterns. It also helps other people understand your data. Four types of graphs that you can use are line graphs, bar graphs, circle graphs, and pictographs.

PURPOSE: In this activity, you will learn how to make different kinds of graphs.

PROCEDURE

Part A: Making a Line Graph

☐ 1. **OBSERVE:** Look at the line graph in Figure 1. Notice that data are plotted as points connected by a line. The horizontal axis shows the range of the independent variable. The vertical axis shows the range of the dependent variable. When graphing, you must decide which values are independent and which are dependent. In Figure 1, the mean temperature depends on the month. Therefore, the mean temperature is the dependent variable, which goes on the vertical axis. The month, the independent variable, is on the horizontal axis.

☐ 2. **GRAPH:** Use the following information and data in Table 1 to create a line graph in the Observations section on page 17.

When meteorologists measure atmospheric pressure, they use a unit called the millibar (mb). Standard air pressure at sea level is 1,013 millibars. The figures in Table 1 describe how air pressure varies with altitude, or height above sea level.

Think about which variable is independent and which is dependent. Remember to include a title and to label the axes. Notice that the lowest air pressure is 3 mb and the highest is 1,013 mb. The air pressure range on your graph should be from 0 mb to just above 1,013 mb.

Monthly Mean Temperature of Seattle, Washington

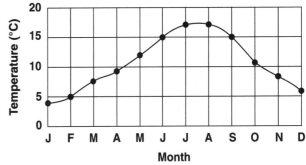

▲ **Figure 1** Line graph

| Table 1: Pressure Changes With Altitude ||
Altitude (km)	Air Pressure (mb)
0	1,013
1.0	899
2.0	795
3.0	701
4.0	617
5.0	540
10.0	265
20.0	55
30.0	12
40.0	3

Part B: Making a Bar Graph

❏ 1. **OBSERVE:** Figure 2 shows a bar graph using the same data as in Figure 1. A bar graph is similar to a line graph except bars rather than points show the data. The bar graph in Figure 2 has the dependent variable on the vertical axis. Bar graphs may also be drawn so that the dependent variable is on the horizontal axis.

❏ 2. **GRAPH:** Use the information in Table 1 on page 15 to create a bar graph in the Observations section. Be sure to label the axes of the graph and to include a title.

Monthly Mean Temperature of Seattle, Washington

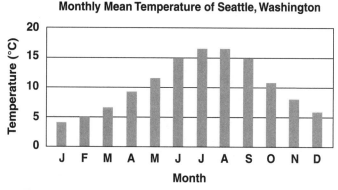

▲ **Figure 2** Bar graph

Part C: Making a Circle Graph

❏ 1. **OBSERVE:** Look at the circle graph shown in Figure 3. You can use a circle graph when your data describe parts of a whole. A circle graph is a circle that is divided into sections. The size of each section shows a percentage of the whole circle. Notice that if you add the percentages of the sections together, they equal 100 percent.

❏ 2. If the data are simple, you can draw a circle graph based on simple fractions of a whole. Suppose you want to graph the fractions of rock types you collected on a field trip: 5 limestone, 10 granite, and 5 sandstone. Since 5 is 1/4 of the total number of rocks, and 10 is 1/2 of the total number of rocks, your graph should look like Figure 4.

❏ 3. **GRAPH:** In the Observations section on page 17, draw a circle graph showing the kinds of fossils found at a dig site. Assume that there are 12 fossils found: 6 saber-toothed cats, 4 giant sloths, and 2 woolly mammoths. Fill in the three sections, using colored pencils to make the graph easier to read. Label the sections and write a title for the graph.

Part D: Making a Pictograph

❏ 1. **OBSERVE:** As the name suggests, a pictograph is a graph using pictures. Look at the pictograph in Figure 5 on page 17. The uses of coal in the United States are represented by the amount of space they occupy on the picture. Figure 6 shows another type of pictograph. In this graph, small pictures represent fossils.

❏ 2. **GRAPH:** Make a pictograph in the Observations section showing types of rocks found in a student's collection. Use the following data for your graph: 2 obsidian, 3 sandstone, 10 quartz, 2 marble, 6 coquina, 5 mica, 3 slate.

Use of Coal in the United States

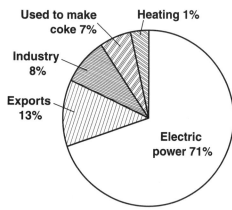

▲ **Figure 3** Circle graph using percentages

Rocks Collected on Field Trip

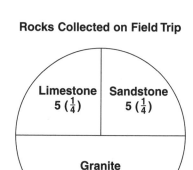

▲ **Figure 4** Circle graph using fractions

LABORATORY SKILLS WORKSHEET 5 *(continued)*

Use of Coal in the United States

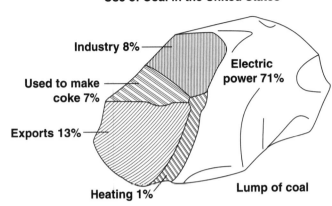

▲ **Figure 5** Pictograph showing percentages

Fossils Found at Three Sites

 = 50 fossils

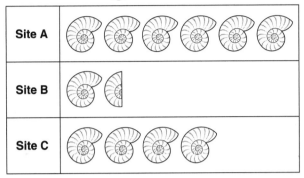

▲ **Figure 6** Pictograph based on numbers

OBSERVATIONS

▲ **Line Graph**

▲ **Bar Graph**

▲ **Circle Graph**

▲ **Pictograph**

CONCLUSIONS

1. What information is presented in the line graph shown in Figure 1? _____

   _____

2. What information is presented along the horizontal axis of Figure 1? _____

3. What information is presented along the vertical axis of Figure 2? _____

4. What is the independent variable in Figure 2? What is the dependent

   variable in Figure 2? _____

5. Look at the line graph in Figure 1. What trend do you see in the mean monthly

   temperature in Seattle? _____

6. How does the bar graph in Figure 2 show this same trend? _____

   _____

7. How would the bar graph shown in Figure 2 look different if the independent
   variable was on the vertical axis instead of on the horizontal axis?

   _____

8. Use the line graph in Figure 1 to determine the mean monthly temperature in

   Seattle in March. _____

9. What information is shown in the circle graph in Figure 3? _____

10. According to Figure 3, how is most of the coal in the United States used?

    What percentage of the total use is this amount? _____

11. According to Figure 3, what is the combined percentage of coal used in the

    United States for heating, industry, and electric power? _____

12. How does a pictograph make data easier to understand compared to using

    only numbers? _____

    _____

LABORATORY SKILLS WORKSHEET 6

Writing a Laboratory Report

Materials

pencil

BACKGROUND: When you perform a laboratory investigation, it is important to keep an organized record of what you do. It is also important to keep an accurate record of your results. An organized record of an investigation is called a laboratory report. A laboratory report is made up of the following sections: Title, Purpose, Background, Hypothesis, Materials, Procedure, Observations, Data, Analysis of Data, and Conclusions.

PURPOSE: In this activity, you will learn how to write a laboratory report.

PROCEDURE

❑ 1. Study the following descriptions of the sections of a laboratory report.

Title—tells about the experiment
Purpose—reason for doing the experiment
Background—information that will help a reader understand the experiment better
Hypothesis—your idea on what you expect the results of the experiment to be
Materials—list of things needed to perform the experiment
Procedure—steps that will be followed during the experiment
Observations—description of what is seen during the experiment
Data—measurements made during the experiment
Analysis of Data—presentation of the data in tables, charts, graphs, or drawings
Conclusions—summary statement of the results; describes whether the data supported the hypothesis and sources of any errors

> A group of students wanted to investigate the porosity of soils, or how easily water soaked through different kinds of soil. They suspected that water would travel through the soils at different rates. In order to test their idea, they constructed four identical setups of empty plastic milk bottles with the tops and bottoms cut off. Each bottle was placed on top of a bucket covered with plastic screening. Each bottle was half filled with one of the types of soil: Bottle A = gravel, Bottle B = sand, Bottle C = peat, Bottle D = clay.
>
> Water from a container was poured through each soil type for a period of 1 minute and collected in the buckets. The students then measured the water from each bucket in a graduated cylinder. They observed that, in 1 minute, 100 mL of water traveled through the gravel; 70 mL through the sand; 30 mL through the peat; and 0 mL through the clay. Based on their results, the students decided that the porosity of the four different soils varies, with gravel having the highest porosity and clay the lowest.

❑ 2. Reread the experiment described above. Write a possible title for the experiment.

_____

❑ 3. Notice the data that the students obtained in the experiment. Make a table to record data for the experiment in the Observations section on page 20.

OBSERVATIONS

CONCLUSIONS

1. State the purpose of this experiment in the form of a question. _____

   _____

2. What was the hypothesis in this experiment? _____

   _____

3. Make a list of materials that the students needed to carry out this experiment.

   _____

   _____

4. What variable was being tested in this experiment? _____

   _____

   _____

5. Write a step-by-step procedure for this experiment. _____

   _____

   _____

   _____

6. Write the conclusion that students reached based on their results. _____

   _____

LABORATORY CHALLENGE FOR LESSON 1-9

How can a three-dimensional landform be modeled from a topographic map?

Materials

lab apron

sheet of cardboard or foam board (at least 30 cm × 30 cm)

pencil or pen

wet sand, clay, or plaster of Paris

spray bottle of water (if using sand)

metric ruler

4 toothpicks

masking tape

BACKGROUND: Different kinds of maps have different purposes. Road maps, for example, show the routes followed by roads to help you find your way from place to place. Such maps almost always show the land as a flat surface. Maps that show the highs and lows of Earth's surface are called relief maps. Topographic maps are relief maps that use contour lines. Because each contour line is drawn through points of equal elevation, these maps show the landscape in three dimensions. With this type of map, you can judge the steepness of the terrain along any given route.

PURPOSE: In this activity, you will model a landform in three dimensions from the information given on a topographic map.

PROCEDURE

Part A: Making Measurements for the Model

☐ 1. **OBSERVE:** Examine the topographic map of the island shown in Figure 1 on page 22.

☐ 2. What is the contour interval used on this map? Record it in Table 1 on page 3.

☐ 3. What are the lowest and highest elevations? Record them in Table 1.

☐ 4. Look at the distance scale on the map. How many meters are represented by 1 cm? Record this number in Table 1.

☐ 5. **CALCULATE:** You will make your model the same length and width as shown on the map. Use the scale and the highest elevation on the map to figure out how tall your model should be. Show your calculations in the space below. Record the number in Table 1.

Part B: Constructing the Model

☐ 1. Lay the map over a sheet of cardboard or foam board.

☐ 2. **MODEL:** Trace the 0 m contour line with a pen or pencil. Press hard enough to make an impression on the cardboard or foam board. Remove the board. This is the base for your model.

☐ 3. **MODEL:** Use wet sand, clay, or plaster of Paris to construct the scale model on the base. If using sand, use a spray bottle of water to keep the sand wet enough to hold its shape. Check that the landscape features are at their correct heights and degrees of steepness.

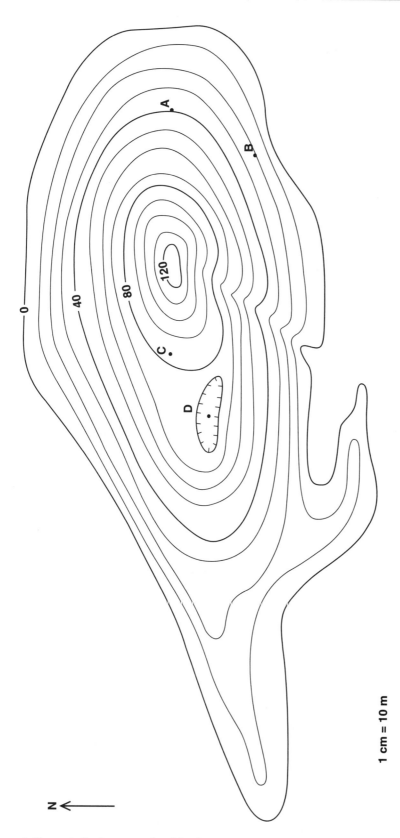

▲ **Figure 1** Contour map of an island

1 cm = 10 m

LABORATORY CHALLENGE FOR LESSON 1-9 *(continued)*

❏ **4.** Use toothpicks and masking tape to make four small flags, as shown in Figure 2. Mark the flags *A, B, C,* and *D.*

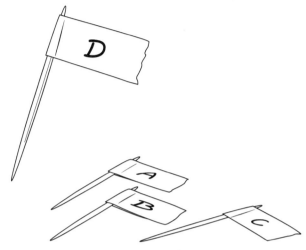

▲ **Figure 2** Make flags for your model.

❏ **5.** Plant the flags on your model in the spots indicated on the map.

❏ **6.** Follow your teacher's instructions for cleaning up your work area.

OBSERVATIONS

Table 1: Map Measurements	
Contour interval	
Lowest elevation	
Highest elevation	
1 cm = ? meters	
Height of model	

CONCLUSIONS

1. What kind of feature is shown at point D?

_____

2. Which flag is at the highest elevation?

_____

3. ANALYZE: When constructing your model, why was it important to use the same scale for height and distance?

_____

_____

CRITICAL THINKING

4. EVALUATE: Look at your landform and identify the location where hiking would be the easiest and where it would be the most difficult. Find these locations on your topographic map. Describe the characteristics of the contour lines at each location.

_____

_____

_____

LABORATORY CHALLENGE FOR LESSON 2-4

How are magnetism, density, and the acid test used to identify minerals?

Materials

safety goggles

lab apron

gloves

samples of quartz, pyrite, magnetite, calcite, and galena

magnet

balance

water

250-mL graduated cylinder

string

petri dish

dropper

dilute hydrochloric acid

BACKGROUND: Magnetism and density are physical properties that can be used to identify minerals. A mineral that is magnetic is attracted to a magnet. Density is sometimes called heft. Density, or heft, describes an object's mass compared to its size. A dense material seems heavy for its size. A less dense material seems light for its size.

Acid can be used to identify a chemical property of certain minerals. The acid test is done by placing a small amount of dilute hydrochloric acid (HCl) on a mineral's surface. The appearance of bubbles indicates that a chemical reaction is taking place. If the mineral begins to bubble, it is calcite, or calcium carbonate ($CaCO_3$).

PURPOSE: In this activity, you will test several minerals for magnetism and for a reaction with dilute hydrochloric acid. You also will calculate the densities of several minerals.

PROCEDURE

Part A: Magnetism

❏ **1.** Put on safety goggles and a lab apron.

❏ **2.** **OBSERVE:** Bring a magnet close to a sample of quartz. If the sample is magnetic, it will be attracted to, or pulled toward, the magnet. If the quartz sample is attracted to the magnet, write *yes* in Table 1 on page 27. If the sample is not magnetic, write *no*.

❏ **3.** Repeat Step 2 for each mineral sample.

Part B: Density

❏ **1.** **MEASURE:** Use the balance to measure the mass of the quartz sample, as shown in Figure 1. Record the mass in the correct column of Table 2.

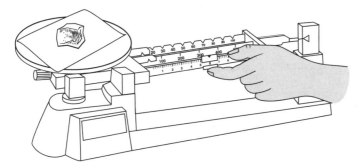

▲ **Figure 1** Measure the mass of the quartz.

❑ 2. Repeat Step 1 for each mineral sample.

❑ 3. **MEASURE:** Fill the graduated cylinder about half full with water. Read the volume of the water to the nearest 0.1 mL.

Write the volume here: _____ mL

❑ 4. **MEASURE:** Tie a piece of string around the quartz sample and carefully lower it into the graduated cylinder. The sample should be completely covered by the water but should not touch the bottom of the graduated cylinder. ⚠ **CAUTION: Be careful not to splash any of the water out of the graduated cylinder.**

❑ 5. **MEASURE:** Read the new volume of water in the graduated cylinder to the nearest 0.1 mL.

Write the new volume here: _____ mL

❑ 6. **CALCULATE:** Calculate the volume of the quartz sample. To find the volume, use the following formula.

Volume of sample = volume of (sample + water) – volume of water

Write the volume of the quartz sample in the appropriate column of Table 2.

❑ 7. Repeat Steps 3–6 for each mineral sample. Make your calculations on a separate sheet of paper.

❑ 8. **CALCULATE:** Calculate the density of each mineral sample. To find the density, use the following formula.

Density = mass ÷ volume

Write the density for each mineral sample in Table 2.

Part C: The Acid Test

❑ 1. Put on gloves. Place the quartz in a petri dish. Use the dropper to place a few drops of dilute hydrochloric acid on the quartz sample. ⚠ **CAUTION: Make sure that the acid is dilute. Be careful not to spill any of the acid on your skin or clothing. If you spill any of the acid, flush the area with water, and notify your teacher immediately.**

❑ 2. **OBSERVE:** Look at the spot where you placed the acid on the quartz. If bubbles form on the spot, write *yes* in Table 3. If no bubbles form, write *no*.

❑ 3. Repeat Steps 1 and 2 for each mineral sample.

❑ 4. Follow your teacher's instructions to dispose of materials and clean up your work area.

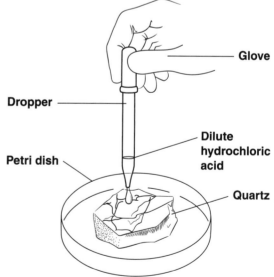

▲ **Figure 2** Place a few drops of dilute hydrochloric acid on the quartz.

LABORATORY CHALLENGE FOR LESSON 2-4 *(continued)*

OBSERVATIONS

Table 1: Magnetism	
Mineral	**Attracted to a Magnet**
Quartz	
Pyrite	
Magnetite	
Calcite	
Galena	

Table 2: Density			
Mineral	**Mass (g)**	**Volume (cm³)**	**Density (g/cm³)**
Quartz			
Pyrite			
Magnetite			
Calcite			
Galena			

Table 3: Acid Test	
Mineral	**Reactions With Acid**
Quartz	
Pyrite	
Magnetite	
Calcite	
Galena	

1. **OBSERVE:** Which mineral was attracted to the magnet? _____

2. **CALCULATE:** Which mineral had the greatest density? _____

3. **CALCULATE:** Which mineral had the least density? _____

4. **COMPARE:** Which minerals had similar densities? _____

   _____

5. **OBSERVE:** Which mineral reacted with the hydrochloric acid? _____

CONCLUSIONS

6. **a. HYPOTHESIZE:** If an unknown mineral is attracted to a magnet, what hypothesis could you state about the mineral?

   _____

   _____

   b. How could you further test this hypothesis?

   _____

   _____

   _____

7. Which of the minerals that you tested could you separate from the others on the basis of its density? Explain your answer.

   _____

   _____

8. **ANALYZE:** What conclusion can you make about the chemical makeup of calcite? On what do you based this conclusion?

   _____

   _____

9. **SUMMARIZE:** Use your observations to state two physical properties and one chemical property for each of the minerals you tested. Describe these properties in Table 4.

Table 4: Properties of Minerals		
Mineral	**Physical Properties**	**Chemical Properties**
Quartz		
Pyrite		
Magnetite		
Calcite		
Galena		

LABORATORY CHALLENGE FOR LESSON 2-5

How is specific gravity measured?

Materials

safety goggles

lab apron

metric ruler

samples of gypsum,
    galena, and pyrite

400-mL graduated
    cylinder

water

spring scale

string

ring stand

burette clamp

BACKGROUND: Specific gravity is a ratio that compares the mass of a substance to the mass of an equal volume of water. The specific gravity of a substance is always the same, no matter what the size of the sample being tested. Because specific gravity is a ratio, specific gravity has no units. It is simply a number.

PURPOSE: In this activity, you will learn how to determine the specific gravity of a substance. Then, you will use this method to calculate the specific gravity of each of several different minerals.

PROCEDURE

☐ **1.** Put on safety goggles and a lab apron. Attach the burette clamp to the ring stand.

☐ **2.** Suspend the spring scale from the burette clamp, as shown in Figure 1.

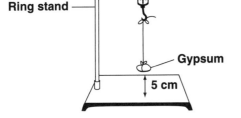

▲ **Figure 1** Suspend the spring scale from the burette clamp.

☐ **3.** Cut a length of string. Tie one end of the string firmly around the sample of gypsum.

☐ **4.** Tie the other end of the string to the spring scale so that the sample hangs 2–5 cm from the bottom of the stand.

☐ **5.** **MEASURE:** Read the mass of the sample of gypsum. Record the mass in the row entitled "Mass in air" in Table 1 on page 31.

☐ **6.** Fill the graduated cylinder about three-quarters full of water.

❏ **7.** Place the gypsum sample into the graduated cylinder so that the gypsum is completely covered by the water, but is not touching the sides or bottom of the cylinder, as shown in Figure 2.

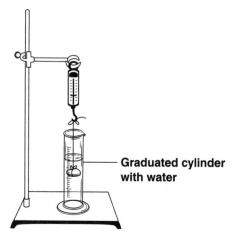

▲ **Figure 2** Suspend the gypsum in the water.

❏ **8. MEASURE:** Read the apparent mass of the sample in water. Record this mass in the row entitled "Mass in water" in Table 1.

❏ **9. CALCULATE:** Calculate the apparent loss of mass by using the following formula.

Apparent loss of mass = mass in air − mass in water

Record the apparent loss of mass in Table 1.

❏ **10.** The apparent loss of mass of the sample in water is equal to the mass of the water the sample displaced. Write the mass of the water displaced in Table 1.

❏ **11. CALCULATE:** Calculate the specific gravity of the sample by using the following formula.

$$\text{Specific gravity} = \frac{\text{mass of mineral in air}}{\text{mass of water displaced}}$$

Record the specific gravity of the gypsum in Table 1.

❏ **12.** Repeat Steps 3–11 for the samples of galena and pyrite.

❏ **13.** Follow your teacher's instructions to clean up your work area.

LABORATORY CHALLENGE FOR LESSON 2-5 (continued)

OBSERVATIONS

Table 1: Calculating Specific Gravity			
Mineral	Gypsum	Galena	Pyrite
Mass in air			
Mass in water			
Apparent loss of mass (mass in air minus mass in water)			
Mass of water displaced			
Specific gravity (mass of mineral in air divided by mass of water displaced)			

1. **COMPARE:** Which mineral had the highest specific gravity?

   _____

2. **COMPARE:** Which mineral had the lowest specific gravity?

   _____

CONCLUSIONS

3. **DESCRIBE:** How is specific gravity measured?

   _____

   _____

   _____

   _____

4. **PREDICT:** If you had equal-sized pieces of galena and pyrite, which would feel heavier? Why?

_____

_____

_____

_____

5. **ANALYZE:** If a piece of gypsum and a piece of pyrite have the same mass, how must the sizes of the pieces compare? Explain your answer.

_____

_____

_____

Name _____ Class _____ Date _____

LABORATORY CHALLENGE FOR LESSON 3-7

How are metamorphic rocks classified?

Materials
safety goggles
lab apron
gloves
labeled samples of:
gneiss
granite
mica schist
slate
shale
sandstone
limestone
quartzite
marble
hand lens
petri dish
dropper
dilute hydrochloric acid

BACKGROUND: Metamorphic rocks form when existing rocks deep within Earth are changed by heat and pressure. Metamorphic rocks can be classified in several ways. One way is according to the minerals that the rocks contain. Another way is according to the rocks from which they were formed.

PURPOSE: In this activity, you will examine some metamorphic rocks and the rocks from which they formed.

PROCEDURE

❑ 1. Put on safety goggles and a lab apron.

❑ 2. **OBSERVE:** Separate the rock samples into metamorphic and nonmetamorphic rocks. Place the two groups on separate sheets of paper. Label the sheets *Metamorphic* and *Nonmetamorphic.*

❑ 3. **OBSERVE:** Look at the samples of gneiss. Describe the appearance of the rock. Record your observations in Table 1 on page 35.

❑ 4. **IDENTIFY:** Examine the gneiss with a hand lens. What minerals do you recognize? Write the names of the minerals in Table 1.

❑ 5. **OBSERVE:** Look at the samples of nonmetamorphic rocks. Choose one that appears to be most like the gneiss. Describe its appearance. Examine it with a hand lens. Try to identify minerals in the rock. Record your observations here:

_____

_____

❑ 6. **COMPARE:** Try to identify the rock you chose that looks the most like gneiss. Record the rock name here:

_____

❑ 7. **COMPARE:** Look at the sample of mica schist. What characteristic do you see in this rock that is similar to gneiss? What do you think is the flaky mineral in the schist? Write your observations in Table 1.

❑ 8. **OBSERVE:** Hold a piece of slate in your hand. Describe the color and feel of this rock. Record your observations in Table 1.

❏ **9. COMPARE:** Look at the samples of nonmetamorphic rocks. Which looks most like slate? Write your choice here:

_____

❏**10. OBSERVE:** Look at a piece of quartzite with a hand lens. Describe the rock's appearance in Table 1.

❏**11. IDENTIFY:** Examine the quartzite further. What mineral is present in this rock? Write your answer in Table 1.

❏**12.** Put on gloves. Place the sample of marble in a petri dish. Use a dropper to place a few drops of dilute hydrochloric acid on the marble. ⚠ **CAUTION: Make sure that the acid is diluted. Be careful not to spill any of the acid on your skin or clothing. If you do spill the acid, flush the area with plenty of water, and notify your teacher immediately.**

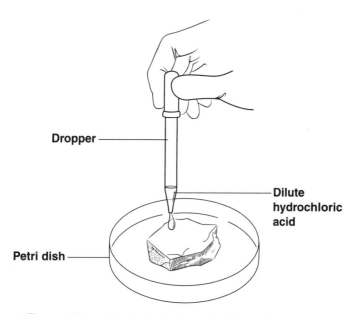

Dropper

Dilute hydrochloric acid

Petri dish

▲ **Figure 1** Place dilute hydrochloric acid on the marble.

❏**13. OBSERVE:** Observe what happens when you place the acid on the marble. Record your observations in Table 1. Which nonmetamorphic rock does marble look like? Add your answer to your observations in Table 1.

❏**14. IDENTIFY:** Use your observations to identify a mineral in the marble. Write your answer in Table 1.

❏**15.** Follow your teacher's instructions to dispose of the acid and clean up your work area. Wash your hands thoroughly.

LABORATORY CHALLENGE FOR LESSON 3-7 *(continued)*

OBSERVATIONS

Table 1: Metamorphic Rocks		
Rock	**Observations**	**Minerals Present**
Gneiss		
Mica schist		
Slate		
Quartzite		
Marble		

1. **CLASSIFY:** Which metamorphic rocks have bands?

_____

_____

2. **INFER:** Which metamorphic rock contains calcite?

_____

3. **COMPARE:** Which sedimentary rock contains the same mineral as quartzite?

_____

CONCLUSIONS

4. **COMPARE:** From what rock is gneiss formed? What observations led to this conclusion?

_____

_____

5. **COMPARE:** From what rock is slate formed? How do you know?

_____

6. **COMPARE:** From what rock is marble formed? How do you know?

_____

_____

7. **COMPARE:** From what rock is quartzite formed? How do you know?

_____

_____

LABORATORY CHALLENGE FOR LESSON 4-4

How can half-life be modeled?

BACKGROUND: Radioactive elements decay at a constant rate. The time it takes for one-half of a radioactive element's isotopes to decay is called the half-life of the element. Different radioactive elements have different half-lives. Some elements decay to stable atoms in less than a second, while others can take millions or even billions of years to decay. When the half-life of a radioisotope is known, this information can be used to find the age of a rock containing that radioisotope.

PURPOSE: In this activity, you will model the decay of a radioactive element.

Materials

- paper
- pencil
- metric ruler
- scissors
- watch or clock with second hand

PROCEDURE

☐ **1.** Draw a 10-cm × 10-cm square on a sheet of paper. Label it *A*. This square represents the original whole sample of radioactive element X. Set square A aside.

☐ **2.** Draw another 10-cm × 10-cm square. Cut out the square. This will be square B. It will represent the decaying process of radioactive element X.

☐ **3.** Record the time at the beginning of the next min.

▲ **Figure 1** Cut out Square B.

_____

This starting time will be equal to 0 sec in Table 1 on page 38. Square B will be equal to one whole sample of radioactive element X, which is about to begin the decay process.

☐ **4.** **MODEL:** Wait 30 sec. Then, carefully cut square B in half as shown in Figure 2. Discard one piece. Have your lab partner record in Table 1 the amount of element X that remains.

☐ **5.** **MODEL:** Wait another 30 sec. Cut the remaining piece of square B in half. Discard one piece. Have your lab partner record the amount of element X that remains.

▲ **Figure 2** Cut Square B in half.

☐ **6.** Repeat Step 5 four more times.

☐ **7.** **COMPARE:** Compare the size of the last piece of paper you cut from square B with the original square A. What part of the whole radioactive sample is the last piece of square B?

Write your answer here: _____

OBSERVATIONS

Table 1: Modeling Radioactive Decay	
Time (in sec)	Amount of Element Remaining
0	1 whole
30	
60	
90	
120	
150	
180	

1. **INTERPRET:** What fraction of radioactive element X remained after the first cut? _____

2. **INTERPRET:** What fraction of radioactive element X remained after the third cut? _____

3. **INTERPRET:** What fraction of radioactive element X remained after the fifth cut? _____

CONCLUSIONS

4. **INTERPRET:** What is the half-life of radioactive element X? _____

5. **CALCULATE:** How much of radioactive element X would remain after 210 sec? Record your calculations in the space below.

6. How can you determine the fraction of radioactive element X that would remain

   after *n* sec? _____

   _____

7. **APPLY:** Radioactive element Y has a half-life of 1,000 years. What fraction of a given amount of element Y will remain after 5,000 years? _____

8. **APPLY:** Potassium-40, an isotope of potassium, decays into argon-40, an isotope of argon. The half-life of potassium-40 is 1.3 billion years. How old is a rock that contains the same amount of potassium-40 and argon-40? Explain your answer.

   _____

   _____

   _____

LABORATORY CHALLENGE FOR LESSON 5-8

How does a seismograph detect and measure earthquake waves?

BACKGROUND: Earthquake waves are detected and measured by an instrument called a seismograph. The record of waves that a seismograph makes is called a seismogram.

PURPOSE: In this activity, you will construct a simple seismograph. Then, you will use your seismograph to record and measure waves made by a model earthquake.

PROCEDURE

Part A: Constructing the Seismograph

❑ **1.** Set up the ring stand and clamp as shown in Figure 1. Place the brick on the base of the ring stand.

❑ **2.** Use the clamp to attach one end of the wooden dowel to the ring stand. Adjust the clamp so that the dowel rests on top of the brick.

❑ **3.** Use heavy string to secure the brick to the wooden dowel.

> ### Materials
> ring stand with clamp
> wooden dowel, about
>   1 m long
> building brick
> heavy string
> scissors
> felt-tipped pen
> small wooden block,
>   about 5 cm × 10 cm
>   × 10 cm
> tape
> roll of adding machine
>   paper

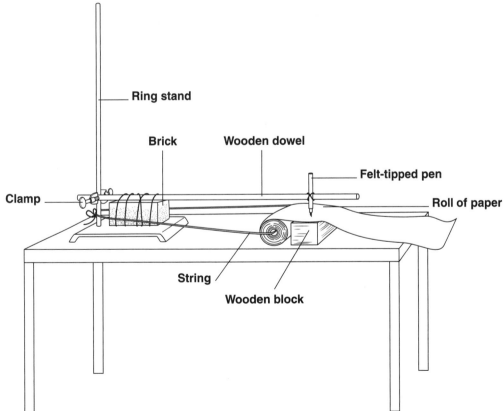

▲ **Figure 1** Setup for seismograph

❏ **4.** Use string to firmly attach a felt-tipped pen to the free end of the wooden dowel, as shown in Figure 2. Make sure that the pen does not wobble when it is touched. Turn the dowel so that the pen is in a vertical position.

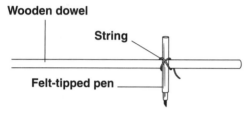

▲ **Figure 2** Attach a felt-tipped pen to the wooden dowel.

❏ **5.** Place the small wood block directly under the pen.

❏ **6.** Cut a piece of string about 2 m long. Pass the string through the hole in a roll of adding machine paper.

❏ **7.** Tie the ends of the string to form a large loop. Loop the string around the rod of the ring stand and position the roll of paper directly behind the wooden block, as shown in Figure 1. The roll of paper will remain in place while the paper strip can still be unrolled.

❏ **8.** Pull the free end of the paper over the wooden block. Loosen the clamp and adjust the height of the pen so that its tip rests lightly on the paper strip. Tighten the clamp with the pen in this position.

Part B: Using the Seismograph

❏ **1.** **OBSERVE:** Pull about 10 cm of the adding machine paper over the wooden block at a constant rate. Do not shake the table or ring stand in any way. Look at the mark made by the pen. Describe the mark in Table 1 on page 41.

❏ **2.** **MODEL:** Pull 20–30 cm of adding machine paper over the wooden block at a constant rate. As you pull the paper, have a partner shake the table gently from side to side. Look at the marks made by the pen. Describe your marks in Table 1.

❏ **3.** Repeat Step 2, but this time have your partner shake the table a little harder.

❏ **4.** Repeat Step 2, this time having your partner shake the table even harder.

Name _____ Class _____ Date _____

LABORATORY CHALLENGE FOR LESSON 5-8 (continued)

OBSERVATIONS

Table 1: Using a Seismograph	
Strength of Shaking	**Seismograph Markings**
None	
Gentle	
Moderate	
Hard	

1. **CONTRAST:** How did the first marking differ from the rest of the markings?

_____

_____

_____

2. **ANALYZE:** How did the markings change as the strength of shaking increased?

_____

_____

_____

3. **MODEL:** What was represented by the shaking table?

_____

CONCLUSIONS

4. **EXPLAIN:** How does a seismograph detect earthquake waves?

_____

_____

_____

5. **APPLY:** How does a seismograph show the strength of earthquake waves?

_____

_____

LABORATORY CHALLENGE FOR LESSON 6-4

How does the thickness of tectonic plates vary?

Concepts and Challenges in Earth Science, Laboratory Manual © Pearson Education, Inc./Globe Fearon/Pearson Learning Group. All rights reserved. Copying strictly prohibited.

BACKGROUND: Tectonic plates are made up of material from Earth's crust and upper mantle. However, these plates vary in thickness because Earth's crust is not the same thickness in all places. The crust can be as thin as 5 km under the oceans and more than 70 km in some continental regions.

PURPOSE: In this activity, you will observe how the thickness of Earth's crust varies from one place to another.

> ### Materials
> safety goggles
> lab apron
> large, clear plastic container
> water
> 4 different-sized wooden blocks
> metric ruler

PROCEDURE

- ☐ 1. Put on safety goggles and a lab apron. Fill a large, plastic container about three-quarters full of water. The water will represent the upper part of the mantle.

- ☐ 2. **MODEL:** Select the largest of four wooden blocks. Let it represent ocean-floor crust. Place the block in the water. Avoid splashing.

- ☐ 3. **MEASURE:** Use a ruler to measure the height of the block above the water. Measure the depth of the block below the water. Record your measurements in Table 1 on page 44.

- ☐ 4. **MODEL:** Take the next largest wooden block and carefully place it on top of the first block. These two blocks together represent a continental plain.

- ☐ 5. **MEASURE:** Use the ruler to measure the height of the two blocks above the water. Measure the depth of the blocks below the water. Record the measurements in Table 1.

- ☐ 6. **MODEL:** Place the larger of the two remaining blocks on top of the first two blocks. The three blocks together represent a low mountain range. Measure the height of the blocks above the water and the depth of the blocks below the water. Record these measurements in Table 1.

- ☐ 7. **MODEL:** Place the smallest block on top of the other three, as shown in Figure 1. Together, these four blocks represent a high mountain range. Measure and record the height and depth of the blocks above and below the water in Table 1.

- ☐ 8. Follow your teacher's instructions for cleaning up your work area.

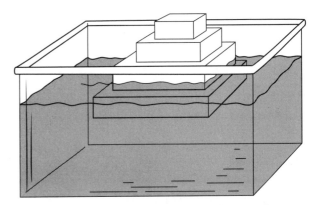

▲ **Figure 1** The four blocks represent a high mountain.

OBSERVATIONS

Table 1: Thickness of Plates of Earth's Crust			
Number of Blocks	Type of Surface Represented	Height Above Water (cm)	Depth Below Water (cm)
1	ocean floor		
2	continental plain		
3	low mountain range		
4	high mountain range		

1. **COMPARE:** When did the least amount of wood extend below the surface of the water? Above the surface of the water?

   _____

2. **COMPARE:** When did the greatest amount of wood extend below the surface of the water? Above the surface of the water?

   _____

CONCLUSIONS

3. **INFER:** Under what part of Earth's surface is the thickness of the plates the greatest?

   _____

4. **HYPOTHESIZE:** Write a hypothesis that states how the thickness of tectonic plates varies for different features of Earth's crust.

   _____

   _____

   _____

Name _____ Class _____ Date _____

How do pore space and porosity affect the movement of water through soil?

Materials
safety goggles
lab apron
clay
sand
gravel
hand lens
paper towel
wax pencil
100-mL beakers (3)
50-mL graduated cylinders (3)
3 cotton wads
100-mL short-stem funnels (3)
3 tripods
water

BACKGROUND: Spaces between soil particles are called pores. The number of pores per unit volume of soil is called porosity. Soil with large and numerous spaces between particles has a high porosity. Soil with fewer and smaller spaces between particles has a low porosity. The porosity of soil affects the way that water moves through the soil.

PURPOSE: In this activity, you will discover how the porosity of soil and the movement of water through soil are related. You also will see how the size of soil particles affects a soil's porosity.

PROCEDURE

Part A: Examining Soil Particles

❏ 1. Put on safety goggles and a lab apron. Place small samples of dry clay, sand, and gravel on a paper towel.

❏ 2. **OBSERVE:** Examine the three soil samples. Observe the size of the particles in each soil type.

❏ 3. Describe the particles in the spaces below.

sand: _____

_____

clay: _____

_____

gravel: _____

_____

❏ 4. **CLASSIFY:** Determine which material has the smallest particles and which has the largest particles. Assign a number to each material based on its particle size. Let the material with the smallest particles be size number 1. Let the material with the largest particles be size number 3. Record the numbers under "Size of Particles" in Table 1 on page 47.

❏ 5. **OBSERVE:** Use a hand lens to examine the three samples more carefully.

❏ 6. **COMPARE:** Which material seems to have the largest pores between particles? Assign number 3 to this material and record it in Table 1 under "Size of Pores."

❏ **7. COMPARE:** Which material seems to have the smallest spaces between particles? Assign number 1 to this material. Assign number 2 to the material with medium-sized pore spaces. Record these sizes in Table 1.

Part B: Speed of Water Through Soil

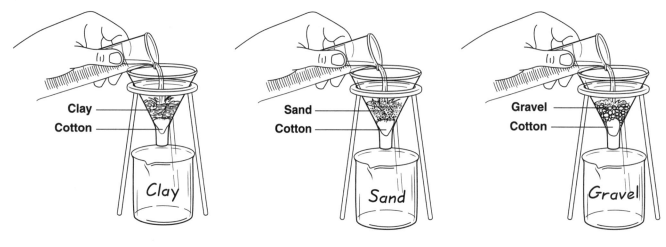

▲ **Figure 1** Water through clay   ▲ **Figure 2** Water through sand   ▲ **Figure 3** Water through gravel

❏ **1.** Using a wax pencil, label three beakers *Clay, Sand,* and *Gravel.* Label three graduated cylinders the same way.

❏ **2.** Roll a small wad of cotton into a ball. Loosely stuff the ball of cotton into a funnel so that it blocks the opening of the stem.

❏ **3.** Place the funnel in a tripod, and put the beaker marked *Clay* under the funnel.

❏ **4.** Half fill the funnel with dry clay.

❏ **5. MEASURE:** Measure 50 mL of water into the graduated cylinder marked *Clay.* Pour the water into the funnel, as shown in Figure 1. Observe how fast the water moves through the funnel into the beaker. Write your observations under "Movement of Water" in Table 2.

❏ **6.** Repeat Steps 2 through 5, using sand and the beaker marked *Sand,* as shown in Figure 2.

❏ **7.** Repeat Steps 2 through 5 again, using gravel and the beaker marked *Gravel,* as shown in Figure 3.

❏ **8. OBSERVE:** How quickly does the water move through the gravel? Does it move faster or slower than it moves through the clay and the sand? Write your observations in Table 2.

❏ **9.** Wait until the water has stopped dripping through all three funnels. Then, pour the water from the beaker marked *Clay* into the graduated cylinder marked *Clay.* Do the same for the sand and the gravel, as shown in Figure 4.

❏ **10. MEASURE:** Measure the water in each graduated cylinder. Record your measurements in Table 2.

▲ **Figure 4** Measure the water that collected in the beaker.

Name _____ Class _____ Date _____

LABORATORY CHALLENGE FOR LESSON 7-4 *(continued)*

OBSERVATIONS

Table 1: Particle Size and Pore Space			
Material	Number Based on Particle Size	Size of Particles	Size of Pores
Sand			
Clay			
Gravel			

Table 2: Water Movement Through Soil		
Soil Type	Movement of Water	Amount of Water Passing Through (mL)
Clay		
Sand		
Gravel		

1. **COMPARE:** Which type of soil—clay, sand, or gravel—has the largest particles?

   _____

2. **COMPARE:** Which type of soil has the smallest particles?

   _____

3. **a.** Which type of soil has the largest pore spaces? _____

   b. The smallest? _____

4. **a.** Through which type of soil did water pass through the fastest? _____

   b. The slowest? _____

5. **a.** Through which type of soil did the most water pass? _____

   b. The least water? _____

CONCLUSIONS

6. **GENERALIZE:** Write a general statement that explains the relationship between particle size and pore space for a soil.

_____

_____

_____

7. **RELATE:** What is the relationship between the particle size for a soil and the rate at which water passes through it?

_____

_____

_____

8. **RELATE:** What is the relationship between the porosity of soil and the amount of water that passes through it?

_____

_____

_____

LABORATORY CHALLENGE FOR LESSON 8-3

What factors affect erosion caused by running water?

BACKGROUND: Running water is the main agent of erosion. As water moves across Earth's surface, it carries away rocks and soil. The amount of erosion caused by moving water depends on different factors.

PURPOSE: In this activity, you will explore some of the factors that affect the ability of running water to cause erosion.

PROCEDURE

Part A: Movement of Materials by Running Water

❏ 1. Put on safety goggles and a lab apron.

❏ 2. Set up a section of rain gutter with one end propped up on a wooden block. The other end of the rain gutter should rest over a sink, as shown in Figure 1. Place a bucket in the sink so that material flowing down the gutter will flow into the bucket. This is your catch bucket.

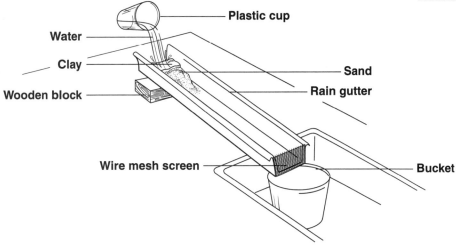

▲ **Figure 1** Set one end of the gutter over a sink.

❏ 3. Fasten a piece of wire mesh screen over the lower end of the gutter.

❏ 4. **MODEL:** Pack some modeling clay into the higher end of the gutter. Add some sand to the gutter just below the clay. This setup will model water moving over base soil on a gentle slope.

❏ 5. **OBSERVE:** Fill a plastic cup with water. Slowly pour the water onto the clay so that the water flows onto the sand. What happens to the sand as the water flows through it? What happens to the sand as it moves down the gutter? Write your observations in Table 1 on page 51.

Materials

safety goggles
lab apron
1-m section of vinyl rain gutter
wooden block
wire mesh screen
modeling clay
sand
water
plastic cup
2 books
dropper
45-cm piece of thin, plastic tube
pinch clamp
3 buckets
grass sod

CHAPTER 8: Erosion   49

❑ **6.** Clean the sand out of the gutter as instructed by your teacher. Increase the slope of the gutter by placing one or two books under the wooden block.

❑ **7.** **MODEL:** Make sure that the modeling clay and wire mesh are still in place. Add some more sand just below the clay. This setup will model water moving over base soil on a steeper slope than before.

❑ **8.** **COMPARE:** Repeat Step 5. Observe what happens to the water and sand. Write your observations in Table 1.

Part B: Effects of Plants on Erosion

❑ **1.** Clean out the gutter as instructed by your teacher.

❑ **2.** Set up the gutter, as shown in Figure 1. Fill the upper end of the gutter with sand.

❑ **3.** **OBSERVE:** Hold a dropper of water about 20 cm above the sand. Allow 15 to 20 drops to fall onto the sand. How does the sand look after water has fallen on it? Record your observations in Table 2.

❑ **4.** **MODEL:** Use plastic tubing, a pinch clamp, and a bucket of water to set up a siphon, as shown in Figure 2.

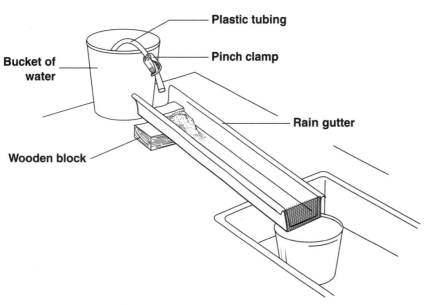

▲ **Figure 2** Set up a siphon.

❑ **5.** **OBSERVE:** Smooth the sand at the top of the gutter. Open the siphon and allow water to run through the sand for about 1 min. Note the speed of the water as it moves through the sand. What happens to the sand as water flows through it? Record your observations in Table 2.

❑ **6.** **OBSERVE:** Look at the water in the catch bucket. Describe the appearance of the water. Record your description in Table 2.

❑ **7.** Remove all the sand from the gutter. Replace the catch bucket with a clean one.

LABORATORY CHALLENGE FOR LESSON 8-3 *(continued)*

☐ **8. MODEL:** Place a piece of grass sod in the upper end of the gutter. Open the siphon and allow water to run onto the sod for about 1 min.

☐ **9. OBSERVE:** Observe the appearance of the sod as the water flows onto it. Also, note the speed of the water as it flows through the sod. How does its speed over the sod compare with its speed as it moved through sand? Record your observations in Table 2.

☐ **10. COMPARE:** How does the appearance of the water in the first catch bucket compare with the water in the second? Write your observations in Table 2.

☐ **11.** Follow your teacher's instructions for cleaning up and putting away equipment. Wash your hands thoroughly.

OBSERVATIONS

Table 1: Elevation and Running Water	
Situation	**Observations**
Water flowing through sand on a shallow slope	
Water flowing through sand on a steeper slope	

Table 2: Sod, Sand, and Erosion by Running Water	
Situation	**Observations**
Water dropped onto sand	
Water running through sand	
Water in first catch bucket	
Water running through sod	
Water in second catch bucket	

1. What happens when running water flows through soil?

   _____

   _____

2. Did the water move faster through the sand or through the grass sod?

   _____

CONCLUSIONS

3. **INFER:** Is erosion by running water greater on a steep slope or on a gentle slope? Explain.

   _____

   _____

4. **INFER:** How does vegetation affect the speed of erosion?

   _____

   _____

5. **INFER:** How does vegetation affect the amount of soil that is washed away by erosion?

   _____

   _____

Name _____ Class _____ Date _____

LABORATORY CHALLENGE FOR LESSON 9-5

What factors affect the speed of a river?

BACKGROUND: Water is added to rivers by heavy rains and by melting ice and snow. Water that does not soak into the ground or evaporate will flow downhill over land and may enter a river. The speed of the water in a river can change as it flows.

PURPOSE: In this activity, you will use a stream table model to find out how the slope of the land affects the speed of water moving over it. You also will find out how adding water affects the speed of a river.

PROCEDURE

Part A: Slope of the Land

❏ 1. Put on safety goggles and a lab apron. Use masking tape to attach a protractor to one side of a section of rain gutter. The straight edge of the protractor should be perpendicular to the bottom of the rain gutter.

❏ 2. Tie a piece of string to a paper clip. Attach the string to the center of the protractor with another piece of tape. The paper clip should hang freely from the protractor, as shown in Figure 1.

❏ 3. Prop one end of a section of rain gutter on a wooden block. Let the other end rest over a sink, as shown in Figure 2.

❏ 4. **MEASURE:** Look at the string on the protractor. It shows the angle of slope of the rain gutter. Record this angle in the correct box of Table 1 on page 55.

Materials
safety goggles
lab apron
masking tape
protractor
1-m section of vinyl rain gutter
string
paper clip
3 wooden blocks
2 buckets
food coloring
45-cm sections of rubber tubing (2)
2 pinch clamps
wax pencil
watch or clock with second hand
paper towels

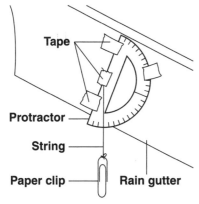

▲ **Figure 1** The paper clip should hang freely from the protractor.

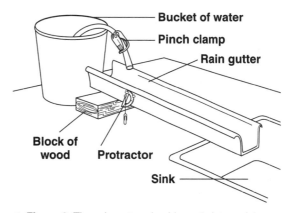

▲ **Figure 2** The rain gutter should empty into a sink.

❏ **5.** Fill a bucket three-quarters full with water. Add food coloring to the water. Place the bucket at the raised end of the rain gutter, as shown in Figure 2.

❏ **6.** Clamp one end of a piece of rubber tubing closed. Submerge the other end of the tubing in the bucket of water to make a siphon. Position the clamped end over the gutter, as shown in Figure 2. ⚠ **CAUTION: Do not attempt to suck water through the tube to make a siphon.**

❏ **7.** Inside the rain gutter, use a wax pencil to make a starting line at the upper end and a finish line at the lower end.

❏ **8.** **MEASURE:** Open the pinch clamp and let the water flow, beginning at the starting line. Use a watch or clock with a second hand to time the flow of the water from the starting line until it reaches the finish line. Record the time in Table 1. Close the siphon.

❏ **9.** **CALCULATE:** Repeat Step 8 two more times. Calculate the average for the three trials and record it in Table 1.

❏**10.** **MEASURE:** Raise the slope of the gutter by placing a second wooden block on top of the first block. Read the angle of the slope on the protractor. Record the angle in Table 1.

❏**11.** Repeat Steps 8 and 9.

❏**12.** Add a third wooden block to the other two blocks. Read the angle of slope. Record the angle in Table 1. Repeat Steps 8 and 9.

❏**13.** Follow your teacher's instructions for cleaning up your work area.

Part B: Amount of Water

❏ **1.** **MODEL:** Set up the stream table model, using one block as in Part A. This time, use two buckets of colored water and two siphons. Position the clamped ends of both siphons over the gutter, as shown in Figure 3.

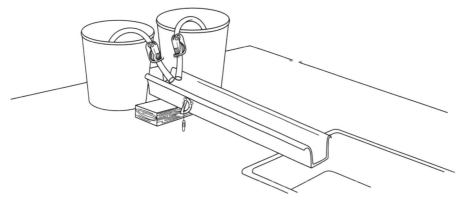

▲ **Figure 3** Use two buckets of water and two siphons.

LABORATORY CHALLENGE FOR LESSON 9-5 *(continued)*

❏ **2.** Make sure that the starting line and finish line are clearly marked on the gutter. Open one pinch clamp to start the water flowing from one siphon.

❏ **3.** **MEASURE:** Use a watch or clock to time the flowing water from the starting line until it reaches the finish line. Record the time in Table 2. Close the siphon.

❏ **4.** Repeat Steps 2 and 3 two more times. Calculate the average for the times. Record the average in Table 2.

❏ **5.** Repeat Steps 2 through 4, this time with both siphons opened. Record your results in Table 2.

❏ **6.** Follow your teacher's instructions to put away materials and clean up your work area.

OBSERVATIONS

Table 1: Slope of the Land					
Wood Blocks	Angle (degrees)	Time (sec)			Average Time (sec)
		Trial 1	Trial 2	Trial 3	
1 block					
2 blocks					
3 blocks					

Table 2: Amount of Water					
Amount of Water	Angle (degrees)	Time (sec)			Average Time (sec)
		Trial 1	Trial 2	Trial 3	
1 siphon flowing					
2 siphons flowing					

1. **COMPARE:** In Part A, which stream had the steepest slope?

   _____

2. **COMPARE:** In Part A, which stream flowed fastest?

   _____

3. **OBSERVE:** In Part B, which stream had more water flowing in it?

   _____

4. **COMPARE:** In Part B, which stream flowed faster?

   _____

CONCLUSIONS

5. **ANALYZE:** How does the slope of the land affect the speed of a river?

   _____

   _____

6. **ANALYZE:** How does the amount of water flowing in a river affect the speed
   of a river?

   _____

   _____

LABORATORY CHALLENGE FOR LESSON 10-3

How do minerals form in ocean water?

Materials

safety goggles
lab apron
100-mL beakers (2)
table salt (NaCl)
stirring rod
2 petri dishes with
    covers
wax pencil
limewater, Ca(OH)$_2$
drinking straw

BACKGROUND: Many elements are dissolved in ocean water. Among these are calcium, chlorine, and sodium. Most of these elements are found as parts of mineral compounds. Calcium hydroxide reacts with carbon dioxide to form solid calcium carbonate. Chlorine and sodium combine to make up sodium chloride.

Two common ways in which solid minerals can form from solutions is by precipitation and by evaporation. Minerals form from precipitation when a solid substance, or precipitate, falls out of solution as the result of a chemical reaction. Evaporation produces a solid mineral when a liquid solvent evaporates, leaving a solid solute behind.

PURPOSE: In this activity, you will discover how precipitation and evaporation cause minerals to form in ocean water.

PROCEDURE

☐ 1. **MEASURE:** Put on safety goggles and a lab apron. Add about 80 mL of water to a 100-mL beaker. Add salt to the water and stir. Continue adding salt until no more salt will dissolve.

☐ 2. Pour the saltwater solution into a petri dish until the dish is about half full.

☐ 3. **OBSERVE:** Observe the solution in the petri dish. Record your observations in the row labeled "Day 1" of Table 1 on page 58.

☐ 4. Put the cover on the petri dish. Use the wax pencil to label it *Salt Water* and set the dish aside.

☐ 5. Add about 80 mL of limewater to a second beaker. Limewater contains calcium hydroxide, Ca(OH)$_2$.

☐ 6. **OBSERVE:** Observe the appearance of the limewater and write your observations in the row labeled "Day 1, before blowing into solution" in Table 2 on page 59.

☐ 7. Place a straw in the limewater and blow gently through the straw, as shown in Figure 1. ⚠ **CAUTION: Do not inhale. Do not swallow any limewater.** You should see bubbles forming in the limewater.

☐ 8. Continue blowing until you see a change in the limewater. Then, continue blowing for about 1 more min. ⚠ **CAUTION: Blow for only a few seconds at a time, taking breaths frequently.**

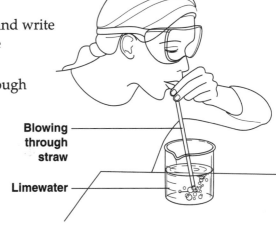

Blowing through straw

Limewater

▲ **Figure 1** Blow into the limewater.

9. **OBSERVE:** What happens to the limewater as you blow into it? Write your observations in the correct box of Table 2.

10. Pour limewater solution into a second petri dish until the dish is about half full. Cover it and label it *Limewater.* Set the dish aside with the dish containing the saltwater solution.

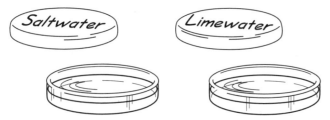

▲ **Figure 2** Place the petri dish covers next to each dish.

11. Remove the petri dish covers and place each cover directly next to the dish to which it belongs, as shown in Figure 2.

12. Let the two petri dishes containing the saltwater and limewater solutions stand undisturbed for 3 days.

13. Follow your teacher's instructions to put away materials and clean up your work area.

14. **OBSERVE:** After 3 days, observe the petri dishes and record any changes that you see. Write your observations in Tables 1 and 2.

OBSERVATIONS

Table 1: Salt Water	
Date	**Observations**
Day 1	
Day 4	

LABORATORY CHALLENGE FOR LESSON 10-3 *(continued)*

Table 2: Limewater	
Date	**Observations**
Day 1, before blowing into solution	
Day 1, after blowing into solution	
Day 4	

1. **COMPARE:** What changes occurred in the saltwater solution after 3 days?

_____

_____

2. **COMPARE:** What changes occurred in the limewater as you blew into it?

_____

_____

3. **COMPARE:** What further changes occurred in the limewater after 3 days?

_____

_____

CONCLUSIONS

4. **IDENTIFY:** What gas entered the limewater as you blew into it?

_____

5. **RELATE:** How does this same gas enter ocean water?

_____

_____

6. **ANALYZE:** What chemical reaction took place between this gas and the limewater?

_____

_____

7. **EXPLAIN:** How does solid salt form along ocean shorelines?

_____

_____

8. **IDENTIFY:** What solid minerals formed in the petri dishes and how did they form?

_____

_____

_____

LABORATORY CHALLENGE FOR LESSON 11-4

Which heats up faster—land or water?

BACKGROUND: Have you walked on sand in your bare feet on a hot, sunny day? If so, you know that the sand is very hot. The sand and water at a beach receive the same amount of energy from the Sun. Yet, the sand may feel very hot, while the water feels much cooler.

PURPOSE: In this activity, you will discover why sand may be hotter than nearby water.

PROCEDURE

☐ **1.** Put on safety goggles and a lab apron. Half fill a 250-mL beaker with sand. Half fill a second 250-mL beaker with water.

☐ **2.** Place each beaker on a ring stand. Using thermometer clamps, position a thermometer inside each beaker. One thermometer should be in the sand and the other in the water, as shown in Figure 1. The thermometers should not be touching the sides or bottoms of the beakers.
⚠ **CAUTION: Be very careful when working with thermometers. They are very fragile.**

☐ **3.** **MEASURE:** Wait until the temperature reading is the same on each thermometer. Record this temperature in the "0 min" column of Table 1 on page 62.

Materials
safety goggles
lab apron
250-mL beakers (2)
sand
water
2 ring stands
2 thermometer clamps
2 thermometers
lamp
watch or clock with second hand
colored pencils

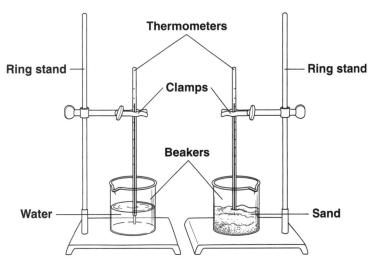

▲ **Figure 1** Clamp the thermometers in place in the water and sand.

❑ **4.** Place a lamp over the two beakers so that both beakers are about 20 cm from the lamp, as shown in Figure 2.

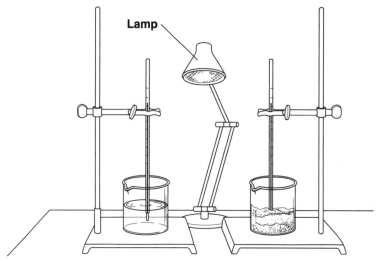

▲ **Figure 2** Both beakers should be about 20 cm from the lamp.

❑ **5.** **MEASURE:** Turn the lamp on. Read the temperature on the thermometer in each beaker every minute for 10 min. Record the temperatures in Table 1.

❑ **6.** **MEASURE:** Turn the lamp off and take it away. Read the temperature of each thermometer. Record the temperatures in the "0 min" column of Table 2 on page 63.

❑ **7.** **MEASURE:** Read the temperature on each thermometer every minute for 10 min. Record the temperatures in Table 2.

❑ **8.** Follow your teacher's instructions to put away materials and clean up your work area.

OBSERVATIONS

Table 1: Heating of Sand and Water											
Time (min)	0	1	2	3	4	5	6	7	8	9	10
Temperature of water (°C)											
Temperature of sand (°C)											

Name _____ Class _____ Date _____

LABORATORY CHALLENGE FOR LESSON 11-4 *(continued)*

Table 2: Cooling of Sand and Water											
Time (min)	0	1	2	3	4	5	6	7	8	9	10
Temperature of water (°C)											
Temperature of sand (°C)											

1. Using the grid in Figure 3, draw a line graph of the results from Table 1. Let the horizontal axis show time in minutes and the vertical axis show temperature in degrees Celsius. Use different colored pencils to graph the lines for water and sand. Label each graph line.

2. Using the grid in Figure 4, draw a line graph of the results from Table 2. Use the same axes and colors that you used for graphing the results from Table 1. Label each graph line.

3. **ANALYZE:** What happened to the temperatures of the soil and water after the lamp was turned on?

_____

Heating of Sand and Water

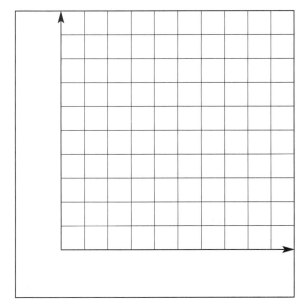

▲ Figure 3

Cooling of Sand and Water

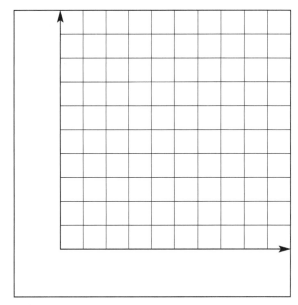

▲ Figure 4

4. COMPARE: How did the change in temperature of the water compare with that of the sand?

_____

_____

5. ANALYZE: What happened to the temperature of the soil and the temperature of the water after the lamp was turned off?

_____

6. COMPARE: Did the temperature of the water and the temperature of the sand change in the same way? Explain.

_____

CONCLUSIONS

7. COMPARE: Which heats up faster—sand or water?

_____

8. COMPARE: Which cools faster—sand or water?

_____

CRITICAL THINKING

9. APPLY: Suppose you went to the beach at night. Which would probably feel cooler—the sand or the water? Explain.

_____

_____

LABORATORY CHALLENGE FOR LESSON 12-1

How can evaporation be speeded up or slowed down?

Concepts and Challenges in Earth Science, Laboratory Manual © Pearson Education, Inc./Globe Fearon/Pearson Learning Group. All rights reserved. Copying strictly prohibited.

BACKGROUND: After it rains, you see puddles of water. Later, the puddles are gone. The water evaporated and changed into a gas. Evaporation can happen quickly or slowly.

PURPOSE: In this activity, you will investigate some factors that can affect the rate at which water evaporates.

PROCEDURE

❑ **1.** Put on safety goggles and a lab apron.

❑ **2.** Cut eight squares, about 3 cm × 3 cm each, from a paper towel. Number the squares 1–8.

❑ **3.** Put on gloves. Pour a small amount of cobalt chloride solution into a beaker. Dip squares 1 and 2 into the beaker of solution, as shown in Figure 1. Paper dipped in cobalt chloride will be pink when it is wet and blue when it dries.

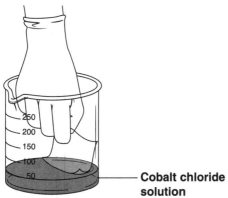

▲ **Figure 1** Dip the squares into the cobalt chloride solution.

❑ **4.** Place the wet squares on separate paper plates and set them aside to dry.
⚠ **CAUTION: If cobalt chloride gets on your hands, wash them immediately.**

❑ **5.** Crumple square 1 and put it back on the plate. Spread square 2 out and place it next to square 1. Set the squares aside for at least 15 min.

Materials
safety goggles
lab apron
gloves
scissors
paper towel
pencil
cobalt chloride solution
100-mL beaker
8 paper plates
lamp
test tube
heat source
test-tube holder
test-tube rack

❑ **6.** Dip squares 3 and 4 into the beaker of cobalt chloride solution. Place each square on a clean paper plate.

❑ **7.** Spread out the two squares. Place square 4 some distance from square 3.

❑ **8.** Position a lamp directly over square 3. Turn the lamp on. Set squares 3 and 4 aside with squares 1 and 2.

❑ **9.** Your teacher will prepare a container of hot water. Pour a small amount of cobalt chloride solution into a test tube. Using a test-tube holder, heat the solution in the test tube by holding it in the hot water. ⚠ **CAUTION: Be very careful when heating the test tube and solution. Keep the test tube pointed away from you and other people.**

❑ **10.** Place the test tube in a rack. Dip square 5 into the warm solution and squeeze out the excess solution. Spread the square out on a clean paper plate.

❑ **11.** Dip square 6 into the cobalt chloride solution that is at room temperature in the beaker. Squeeze as much solution out of it as you can. Spread square 6 out on a clean paper plate next to square 5. Set squares 5 and 6 aside with the other squares.

❑ **12.** **OBSERVE:** After squares 1 and 2 have set for at least 15 min, record the color of each square in rows 1 and 2 of Table 1 on page 67.

❑ **13.** **COMPARE:** After 15 min, look at squares 3 and 4. Note which square is warmer. Also note the color change of each square. Record your observations in rows 3 and 4 of Table 1.

❑ **14.** **OBSERVE:** After squares 5 and 6 have set for at least 15 min, record the color change of each square in rows 5 and 6 of Table 1.

❑ **15.** Dip squares 7 and 8 into the beaker of cobalt chloride solution. Squeeze out the excess solution from both. Spread square 7 out on a clean paper plate.

❑ **16.** Hold square 8 by one edge and wave it back and forth for a couple of minutes.

❑ **17.** **OBSERVE:** Examine squares 7 and 8 to see what color each shows. Record your observations in rows 7 and 8 of Table 1.

❑ **18.** Follow your teacher's instructions to put away materials and clean up your work area. Wash your hands thoroughly.

Name _____ Class _____ Date _____

LABORATORY CHALLENGE FOR LESSON 12-1 *(continued)*

OBSERVATIONS

Table 1: Speed of Evaporation	
Square	**Observations**
1 (crumpled)	
2 (spread out)	
3 (lamp)	
4 (no lamp)	
5 (warm)	
6 (room temperature)	
7 (left on table)	
8 (waved in air)	

1. **COMPARE:** Which square (1 or 2) had more surface area exposed to the air? _____

2. **COMPARE:** Which square (1 or 2) dried faster? _____

3. **IDENTIFY:** Which square (3 or 4) was exposed to light and heat? _____

4. **COMPARE:** Which square (3 or 4) dried faster? _____

5. **IDENTIFY:** Which square (5 or 6) was dipped in warm solution? _____

6. **COMPARE:** Which square (5 or 6) dried faster? _____

7. **IDENTIFY:** Which square (7 or 8) was moved through the air? _____

8. **COMPARE:** Which square (7 or 8) dried faster? _____

CONCLUSIONS

9. **RELATE:** How does surface area affect the speed of evaporation?

_____

_____

10. **ANALYZE:** How do heat and light affect the speed of evaporation?

_____

11. **ANALYZE:** How does the temperature of a liquid affect the speed of evaporation?

_____

12. **ANALYZE:** How does moving air, or wind, affect the speed of evaporation?

_____

13. **APPLY:** List four factors that can affect the speed of evaporation.

_____

_____

Name _____ Class _____ Date _____

How does the greenhouse effect contribute to global warming?

Materials

2 clear plastic shoeboxes

clear plastic shoebox lid

wax pencil

2 thermometers

metric ruler

2 colored pencils

BACKGROUND: The beginning of the Industrial Revolution marked a dramatic increase in the burning of fossil fuels. This practice has resulted in great amounts of carbon dioxide gas being added to Earth's atmosphere over the past 150 years. Carbon dioxide in the atmosphere acts much like glass in a greenhouse. When radiation from the Sun passes through the glass of a greenhouse, it is absorbed by soil and plants and changed to heat energy. This heat energy cannot pass through the glass and is trapped inside the greenhouse. Like the glass, carbon dioxide gas in the atmosphere traps heat from Earth's surface and keeps it from escaping back into space.

PURPOSE: In this activity, you will model the greenhouse effect and examine some causes and consequences of global warming.

PROCEDURE

Part A: Modeling the Greenhouse Effect

☐ **1.** Use a wax pencil to label one plastic shoebox *A* and the other shoebox *B*. Place the two shoeboxes next to each other in direct sunlight.

☐ **2.** Place a thermometer in the center of each shoebox.

☐ **3.** **MEASURE:** Observe the temperature reading of each thermometer. Record the temperatures in the boxes beside "0 min" in Table 1 on page 70.

☐ **4.** **MODEL:** Place the lid on shoebox B, as shown in Figure 1. This model will represent a layer of Earth's atmosphere containing a high percentage of carbon dioxide gas.

☐ **5.** **MEASURE:** Read the temperature of each thermometer after 5, 10, and 15 min. Record the readings in Table 1.

☐ **6.** **CALCULATE:** For each shoebox, subtract the temperature at 0 min from the temperature at 15 min. The result will be the total temperature increase. Record your results in Table 1.

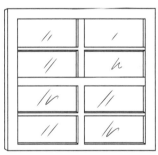
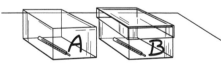

▲ **Figure 1** Place a lid on shoebox B.

Part B: Graphing the Results

☐ **1.** **COMPARE:** Use the graph paper in Figure 2 to graph the results of your experiment. Use two different colored pencils to draw line graphs of the temperature changes in shoeboxes A and B.

☐ **2.** Label the horizontal axis, or *x*-axis, *Time in Minutes*. Mark this axis in even units from 0 to 20. Label the vertical axis, or *y*-axis, *Temperature in Degrees Celsius*. Mark this axis in equal units from 0 to 20.

☐ **3.** Provide a key to identify which color you will use for each shoebox.

OBSERVATIONS

Table 1: Changes in Temperature		
Time	Shoebox A Temperature (°C)	Shoebox B Temperature (°C)
0 min		
5 min		
10 min		
15 min		
Total temperature increase		

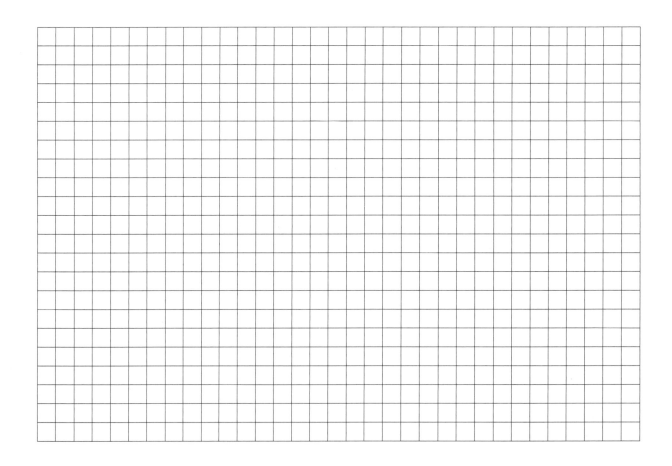

▲ **Figure 2** Graph paper

LABORATORY CHALLENGE FOR LESSON 13-4 *(continued)*

CONCLUSIONS

1. **COMPARE:** Was there any difference between shoebox A and shoebox B in the amount of heat received from the Sun?

   _____

2. **COMPARE:** In which shoebox was the temperature increase greater? Explain.

   _____

   _____

   _____

3. **ANALYZE:** Examine the graph in Figure 3. It shows the relationship between carbon dioxide in the atmosphere and fossil fuel emissions. Over the past 150 years, what has happened to the carbon dioxide concentration in the atmosphere as carbon dioxide emissions from burning fossil fuels increased?

   _____

   _____

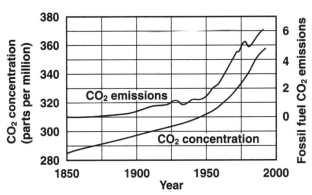

▲ **Figure 3** CO_2 Concentration and Fossil Fuel Emissions

4. **INFER:** The graph in Figure 4 shows changes in the level of carbon dioxide in the atmosphere over the past 1,000 years. About when did the carbon dioxide concentration begin to rise significantly? What was the major cause of this increase?

_____

_____

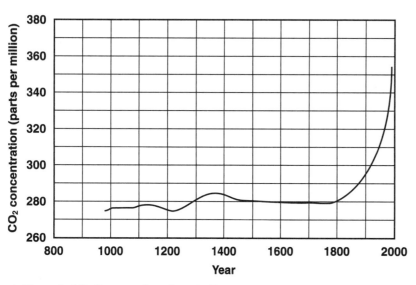

▲ **Figure 4** CO_2 Concentrations Over the Past 1,000 Years

CRITICAL THINKING

5. **PREDICT:** What prediction can you make about the level of carbon dioxide in Earth's atmosphere beyond 2000? What effect will this likely have on the atmosphere?

_____

_____

_____

6. **APPLY:** What are some things that people can do to decrease the greenhouse effect?

_____

_____

_____

_____

LABORATORY CHALLENGE FOR LESSON 14-4

How can you track the Sun's movement across the sky?

Materials

atlas or almanac

piece of heavy
  white paper
  (30 cm × 20 cm)

piece of cardboard
  (40 cm × 40 cm)

drawing compass

protractor

ruler or straightedge

masking tape

modeling clay

plastic drinking straw

magnetic compass

BACKGROUND: Every day, the Sun seems to rise in the east, travel across the sky, and set in the west. This apparent motion of the Sun is caused by Earth's rotation. Since the beginning of time, people have used these motions to mark the passage of time. One device used for this purpose is a sundial.

PURPOSE: In this activity, you will make a simple sundial that will allow you to make a record of the Sun's changing position in the daytime sky.

PROCEDURE

☐ 1. **LOCATE:** Use an atlas or almanac to find the latitude of your community to the nearest 5°. You will use this information to make your sundial.

☐ 2. Using a drawing compass, draw a semicircle with a diameter of 20 cm on a piece of heavy white paper, as shown in Figure 1. ⚠ **CAUTION: Be careful when using the compass. The point on which the compass turns is very sharp.**

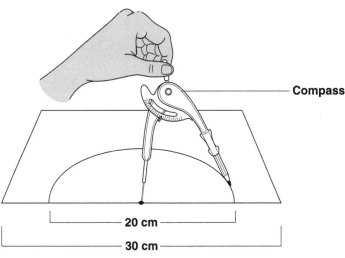

— Compass

├── 20 cm ──┤

├──── 30 cm ────┤

▲ **Figure 1** Draw a semicircle with a diameter of 20 cm.

☐ 3. **MEASURE:** Place a protractor on the diameter of the semicircle and measure angles at 30° intervals, starting at 0° and ending at 180°. Use tic marks to indicate each angle, as shown in Figure 2 on page 74.

☐ 4. Using a ruler or other straightedge, draw lines from the center of the diameter through each tic mark to the edge of the semicircle.

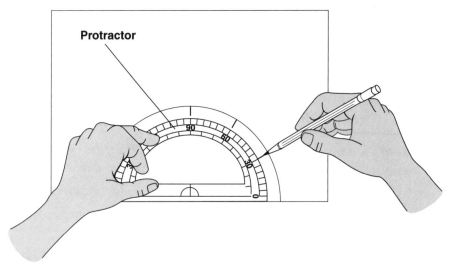

▲ **Figure 2** Measure angles at 30° intervals.

❑ **5.** Use masking tape to attach the white paper to a larger piece of cardboard.

❑ **6.** Place a small lump of modeling clay at the center of the diameter of the semicircle. Insert a plastic drinking straw into the clay. Tilt the straw so that the top of the straw is leaning toward the circumference of the semicircle, as shown in Figure 3.

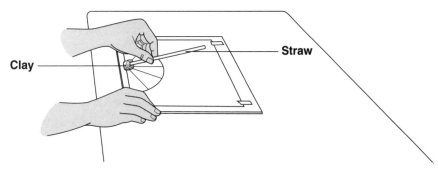

▲ **Figure 3** Tilt the straw toward the circumference of the semicircle.

❑ **7.** Using the protractor, adjust the angle of the straw's tilt to match the latitude of your community, as shown in Figure 4 on page 75.

❑ **8.** Carefully carry your sundial to a location where it can be placed in direct sunlight all day. Using a magnetic compass, arrange the sundial so that the straw lines up in a north-south direction, with the elevated tip of the straw pointing north.

LABORATORY CHALLENGE FOR LESSON 14-4 (continued)

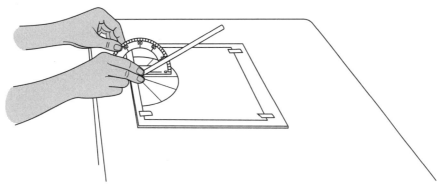

▲ **Figure 4** Adjust the straw's tilt to match your community's latitude.

☐ 9. **OBSERVE:** Check the time. When the clock reads on the hour, such as 10:00 A.M., observe the shadow of the straw. Use a pencil to mark the position of the shadow. Label the mark *1*. Record the time, date, and observations for mark *1* in Table 1.

☐10. Return to your sundial every hour on the hour throughout the day. Mark and number each position of the straw's shadow and record the times, dates, and observations in Table 1. You may wish to record the hourly shadow positions for several consecutive days.

OBSERVATIONS

Table 1: Tracking the Sun's Motion		
Clock Time	**Mark #**	**Observations**
1		
2		
3		
4		
5		
6		
7		
8		

1. **OBSERVE:** About how many degrees does the Sun's shadow move each hour?

   _____

2. **COMPARE:** At which numbered marked is the shadow of the Sun at its highest point?

   _____

3. What is the clock time that corresponds with this mark?

   _____

CONCLUSIONS

4. **COMPARE:** The shadow of the Sun will be at its highest point at noon solar time. At your location, how does noon solar time compare with noon clock time?

   _____

   _____

5. **INFER:** Why do you think that solar time and clock time are not exactly the same?

   _____

   _____

6. **ANALYZE:** Can you accurately measure the passage of hours, using solar time? Explain.

   _____

   _____

   _____

LABORATORY CHALLENGE FOR LESSON 15-9

How can hard water be softened?

BACKGROUND: As groundwater passes through rocks and other materials, minerals may become dissolved in the water. Two minerals often dissolved in groundwater are salts of calcium and of magnesium. Water containing a large amount of dissolved minerals is called hard water. You can tell that water is hard if it is difficult to form suds in the water.

Hard water can be temporary or permanent. Temporary hard water can be softened by heating. Permanent hard water cannot be softened by heating. It can be softened only by adding chemicals to the water.

PURPOSE: In this activity, you will soften both temporary and permanent hard water.

PROCEDURE

❑ **1.** Put on safety goggles and a lab apron.

❑ **2.** Half fill a test tube with distilled water. Use a marking pen to label this test tube *A*.

❑ **3.** Using a dropper, add 3 drops of liquid soap to test tube A, as shown in Figure 1.

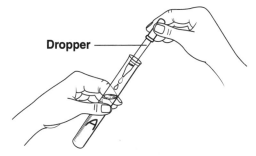

Dropper

▲ **Figure 1** Add liquid soap to test tube A.

❑ **4. OBSERVE:** Put a stopper on the test tube and shake it for 10 seconds, as shown in Figure 2. What do you observe in the test tube? Write your observations in Table 1 on page 79.

❑ **5.** Half fill two test tubes with calcium carbonate solution. Label these test tubes *B* and *C*. Place test tube C in the test-tube rack.

Materials
safety goggles
lab apron
5 test tubes
distilled water
marking pen
dropper
liquid soap
5 rubber stoppers
saturated calcium carbonate solution
test-tube rack
test-tube clamp
250-mL beaker
water
heat source
magnesium chloride
borax

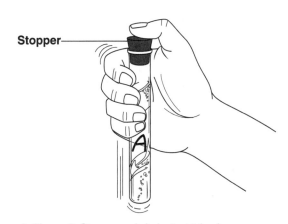

Stopper

▲ **Figure 2** Stopper and shake test tube A.

☐ **6.** **OBSERVE:** Add 3 drops of liquid soap to test tube B. Place a stopper in the test tube and shake the tube for 10 seconds. Look at the liquid in the test tube and write your observations in Table 1. Place the test tube in the test-tube rack.

☐ **7.** Add about 200 mL of water to a 250-mL beaker. Place the beaker on a heat source and turn it on. ⚠ **CAUTION: Always be careful when working with heat.**

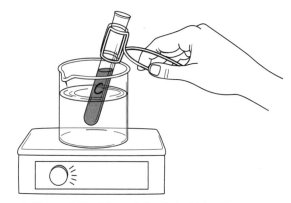

☐ **8.** Remove test tube C from the test-tube rack. Using a test-tube clamp, hold the test tube in the beaker of water that is being heated, as shown in Figure 3. ⚠ **CAUTION: Do not point the open mouth of the test tube toward yourself or anyone else while it is being heated.** Remove the test tube from the water when the calcium carbonate solution in the tube begins to boil.

▲ **Figure 3** Heat the solution in test tube C.

☐ **9.** Set the heated test tube back in the test-tube rack and allow it to cool. Turn off the heat source.

☐**10.** Half fill the two remaining test tubes with distilled water. Label these test tubes *D* and *E*. Dissolve a small amount of magnesium chloride in the distilled water of each of these test tubes. Place test tube E in the test-tube rack.

☐**11.** **OBSERVE:** Add 3 drops of liquid soap to test tube D. Put a stopper on the test tube and shake it for 10 seconds. Observe the test tube. Write your observations in Table 1.

☐**12.** Add a small amount of borax to test tube E. Then, add 3 drops of liquid soap to the mixture in the test tube.

☐**13.** **OBSERVE:** Place a stopper on test tube E, containing the borax, soap, and magnesium chloride. Shake the test tube for 10 seconds. Observe the test tube and record your observations in Table 1.

☐**14.** After test tube C has cooled, add 3 drops of liquid soap to the test tube.

☐**15.** **OBSERVE:** Put a stopper on the test tube and shake it for 10 seconds. Write your observations in Table 1.

☐**16.** Follow your teacher's instructions for cleanup and disposal of waste materials.

Name _____ Class _____ Date _____

LABORATORY CHALLENGE FOR LESSON 15-9 *(continued)*

OBSERVATIONS

Table 1: Softening Hard Water	
Type of Water	**Observations**
Distilled water (test tube A)	
Calcium carbonate solution (test tube B)	
Calcium carbonate solution; heated, then cooled (test tube C)	
Magnesium chloride solution (test tube D)	
Magnesium chloride solution and borax (test tube E)	

1. **COMPARE:** In which types of water did little or no suds form?

   _____

   _____

2. **COMPARE:** In which of the calcium carbonate solutions did more soap suds form?

   _____

   _____

3. **COMPARE:** How did the reaction of magnesium chloride solution containing borax compare to that of the magnesium chloride solution without borax when soap was added to each?

   _____

   _____

CONCLUSIONS

4. ANALYZE: What minerals may cause temporary hard water?

_____

5. APPLY: How can temporary hard water be softened?

_____

6. ANALYZE: What minerals may cause permanent hard water to form?

_____

7. APPLY: How can permanent hard water be softened?

_____

_____

CRITICAL THINKING

8. APPLY: How could you test the water in your home to determine if it is hard water or soft water?

_____

_____

9. APPLY: If your home has hard water, how can you determine if the water is temporary hard water or permanent hard water?

_____

_____

LABORATORY CHALLENGE FOR LESSON 16-7

How does a heat shield work?

BACKGROUND: In a space vehicle like the space shuttle, insulation in the form of a heat shield is needed to protect both the vehicle and the astronauts from extremely high temperatures when the space vehicle reenters the Earth's atmosphere. The space shuttle uses ceramic tiles that can withstand temperatures of nearly 3,000°F.

PURPOSE: In this challenge, you will demonstrate how a heat shield works.

PROCEDURE

- ☐ **1.** Put on safety goggles and a lab apron.

- ☐ **2.** Cut 5 pieces of aluminum foil, each approximately 30 cm × 30 cm. Cover the outside of a paper cup with one piece of aluminum foil. Using a felt-tip pen, label this cup *A* and set it aside.

- ☐ **3.** Cover the outside of a second paper cup with a piece of paper towel. Mold the paper towel to fit the shape of the cup and fold it over the top edge of the cup, as shown in Figure 1.

- ☐ **4.** Over the paper towel on the second cup, place two layers of aluminum foil. Mold the foil to the shape of the cup. Then, wrap another layer of paper towel over the foil.

- ☐ **5.** Cover this second layer of paper towel with two more layers of aluminum foil. Mold the foil to the shape of the cup. If necessary, tape the foil in place at the top edge of the cup. Label this cup *B*.

- ☐ **6.** Fill each cup about three-quarters full of water. Set each cup on a heat source.

- ☐ **7.** Use clamps to attach each of two thermometers to its own ring stand. ⚠ **CAUTION: Handle thermometers carefully.** Position the ring stands so that the thermometer bulbs are in the water inside each cup, as shown in Figure 2 on the next page. Do not let the thermometer touch the sides or bottom of the cups.

- ☐ **8.** **MEASURE:** Read the thermometer in each cup. Record the temperatures in Table 1 on page 80 under "0 min."

- ☐ **9.** Turn on the heat sources and carefully heat the water in the cups. ⚠ **CAUTION: Observe all safety rules when using a heat source.**

- ☐ **10.** **MEASURE:** After 1 min, turn off the heat sources and record the temperature of the water in each cup. Record your measurements in Table 1.

Materials

safety goggles
lab apron
scissors
aluminum foil
metric ruler
2 large paper cups
felt-tip pen
paper towels
masking tape
water
2 heat sources
2 ring stands with clamps
2 thermometers
clock or watch with second hand
2 burette clamps

▲ **Figure 1** Wrap a cup in a paper towel.

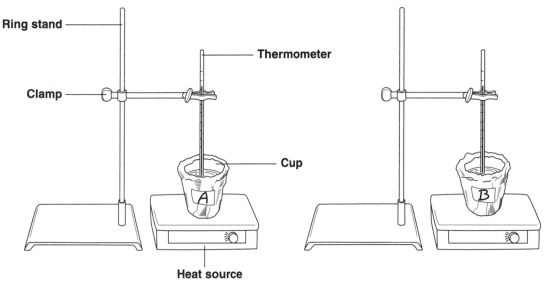

Ring stand

Thermometer

Clamp

Cup

A

B

Heat source

▲ **Figure 2** Attach the thermometers to the ring stands.

OBSERVATIONS

Table 1: Observing a Heat Shield		
	Temperature (°C)	
Cup	0 min	1 min
A		
B		

1. **OBSERVE:** How much did the temperature of the water increase in cup A? _____

2. **OBSERVE:** How much did the temperature of the water increase in cup B? _____

CONCLUSIONS

3. **RELATE:** In which cup was the water protected from heat outside the cup? _____

4. **INFER:** In this investigation, what materials served as a heat shield?

_____

5. **COMPARE:** How is the cup's heat shield similar to a space shuttle's heat shield?

_____

_____

_____

LABORATORY CHALLENGE FOR LESSON 17-1

How can a scale model of the solar system be made?

Materials

pencil

string

meterstick

scissors

2 sheets of paper
   (about 1.5 m × 1.5 m)

drawing compass

BACKGROUND: A scale model shows relative sizes of objects. A scale model also can show the relative distances among objects. Can you make a scale model of the planets that shows both their relative diameters and their relative distances from the Sun?

PURPOSE: In this activity, you will compare the sizes of the planets and their distances from the Sun. You also will discover some of the problems that result when trying to make a scale model of the solar system.

PROCEDURE

☐ **1.** Look at Table 1 on page 85. Using the scale 1 cm = 10,000 km, calculate the scale diameter of the Sun. You can find the scale diameter easily by moving the decimal point in the actual measurement four places to the left.

> diameter of the Sun = 1,392,000 km

> scale diameter = 139.2 cm

Write the scale diameter of the Sun in Table 1.

☐ **2. CALCULATE:** Using the scale 1 cm = 10,000 km, calculate the scale diameter for each planet. Round your answers to the nearest 0.1 cm. Write these measurements in Table 1.

☐ **3. CALCULATE:** Using the scale 1 cm = 10,000 km, calculate the scale distance from the Sun for each planet. Round your answers to the nearest 100 cm. Write these measurements in Table 1.

☐ **4.** Tie a pencil to one end of a piece of string. Starting at the pencil, measure and cut the string so that its length is one-half of the scale diameter of the Sun. This is the scale radius of the Sun.

❑ 5. **MODEL:** As shown in Figure 1, use the pencil and string like a compass to draw a circle equal in diameter to the scale diameter of the Sun. (Remember that the radius of a circle is equal to half its diameter.) To make the circle, have a lab partner hold the end of the string down in the center of one of the sheets of paper. This will be the center of the circle that represents the Sun.

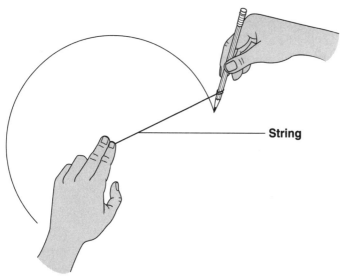

String

▲ **Figure 1** Draw a circle that represents the Sun.

❑ 6. Stretch the string out taut over the paper. Hold the pencil vertically with its point touching the paper. While you trace the circle, your partner should hold down the string, turning the fingers so that they point to and move with the pencil.

❑ 7. Use scissors to cut out the circle. ⚠ **CAUTION: Always be careful when using scissors.** Label the circle *Sun.*

❑ 8. Repeat Steps 4–7 for each planet, using a drawing compass to draw your circles. Label each circle with the name of the planet it represents.

LABORATORY CHALLENGE FOR LESSON 17-1 *(continued)*

OBSERVATIONS

Table 1: Dimensions of Solar System				
Sun/Planet	Diameter (km)	Scale Diameter (cm)	Average Distance From Sun (km)	Scale Distance (cm)
Sun	1,392,000	139.2	_____	_____
Mercury	4,878		57,000,000	
Venus	12,104		108,000,000	
Earth	12,756		150,000,000	
Mars	6,794		228,000,000	
Jupiter	143,884		778,000,000	
Saturn	120,536		1,427,000,000	
Uranus	51,118		2,870,000,000	
Neptune	50,538		4,497,000,000	
Pluto	2,324		5,900,000,000	

1. **COMPARE:** How does the diameter of the largest planet compare with the diameter of the Sun?

   _____

   _____

2. **COMPARE:** How does the diameter of the smallest planet compare with the diameter of the largest planet?

   _____

   _____

3. **CALCULATE:** Look at the scale distance of Mercury from the Sun. Express this distance in meters.

   _____

4. What is the scale distance of Pluto from the Sun? Express this distance in meters.

_____

CONCLUSIONS

5. ANALYZE: Can you construct a model of the solar system that uses scale models of the planets to compare their sizes? Explain.

_____

6. ANALYZE: Can you construct a scale model of the solar system that shows accurately the relative distances of the planets from the Sun as well as the sizes of the planets? Why or why not?

_____

_____

_____

_____

CRITICAL THINKING

7. ANALYZE: To construct the scale model described in question 6, would it help to use a different scale, such as 1 cm = 1 million km? Explain.

_____

_____

LABORATORY CHALLENGE FOR LESSON 18-2

How can light from stars be studied?

Concepts and Challenges in Earth Science, Laboratory Manual © Pearson Education, Inc./Globe Fearon/Pearson Learning Group. All rights reserved. Copying strictly prohibited.

Materials

diffraction grating

assorted colored pencils
  or markers

incandescent lamp

fluorescent lamp

gas vapor tubes (sodium,
  neon, hydrogen)

BACKGROUND: When white light passes through a diffraction grating, it is broken up into the colors of the visible spectrum. When a body such as a star gives off light, the colors in the light's spectrum vary according to the elements that are present in the star. This happens because the light given off by each element has a characteristic wavelength. Each wavelength produces a different color. If a certain color is missing from a star's spectrum, you know that the corresponding element is not present in the star.

PURPOSE: In this activity, you will use a diffraction grating to observe light from different sources. You will also see how elements can be identified by their spectra.

PROCEDURE

☐ **1.** Hold up a diffraction grating and look at a bright part of the sky.
   ⚠ **CAUTION: Never look directly at the Sun.**

☐ **2.** **OBSERVE:** Move the diffraction grating in front of your eyes until you see a spectrum form on the grating. Use colored pencils or markers to make a drawing of this spectrum in the space labeled Diagram 1.

▲ **Diagram 1** Spectrum: light from sky

☐ **3.** **OBSERVE:** Turn on an incandescent lamp. Hold the diffraction grating in front of the lamp, as shown in Figure 1, and observe the spectrum. Draw the spectrum in the space labeled Diagram 2. Turn off the lamp.

▲ **Figure 1** Observe the spectrum produced by light from an incandescent lamp.

▲ **Diagram 2** Spectrum: incandescent lamp

❏ **4. OBSERVE:** Turn on a fluorescent lamp. Observe the light through the diffraction grating. Make a drawing of what you see in the space labeled Diagram 3. Turn off the lamp.

▲ **Diagram 3** Spectrum: fluorescent lamp

❏ **5. OBSERVE:** Look through the diffraction grating at a lighted sodium vapor tube, as shown in Figure 2. In the space labeled Diagram 4, draw the spectrum that you see.

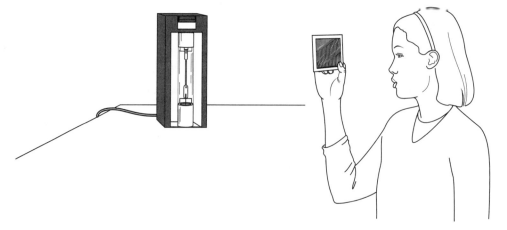

▲ **Figure 2** Observe the spectrum produced by light from a sodium vapor tube.

Name ______________________ Class ______________ Date ______________

LABORATORY CHALLENGE FOR LESSON 18-2 *(continued)*

▲ **Diagram 4** Spectrum: sodium

❑ 6. **OBSERVE:** Look through the diffraction grating at a lighted neon vapor tube. In the space labeled Diagram 5, draw the spectrum that you see.

▲ **Diagram 5** Spectrum: neon

❑ 7. **OBSERVE:** Look through the diffraction grating at a lighted hydrogen vapor tube. In the space labeled Diagram 6, draw the spectrum that you see.

▲ **Diagram 6** Spectrum: hydrogen

OBSERVATIONS

1. **OBSERVE:** What does a diffraction grating do to light? _____

    _____

2. **COMPARE:** How does the spectrum from an incandescent lamp compare with the spectrum of natural light?

    _____

    _____

    _____

3. **CONTRAST:** How is the spectrum from a fluorescent lamp different from the spectrum from an incandescent lamp?

    _____

    _____

4. **CONTRAST:** How are spectra from the sodium, neon, and hydrogen vapor tubes different from the spectra from the lamps?

    _____

    _____

CONCLUSIONS

5. **ANALYZE:** What is the characteristic spectrum for the element sodium? _____

6. **ANALYZE:** What is the characteristic spectrum for the element neon? _____

7. **ANALYZE:** What is the characteristic spectrum for the element hydrogen? _____

8. **ANALYZE:** What information can a diffraction grating give about a star? _____

    _____

    _____

    _____

    _____

Notes

Notes